Water

Resources

Water

David Lewis Feldman

polity

First published in 2012 by Polity Press

Polity Press
65 Bridge Street
Cambridge CB2 1UR, UK

Polity Press
350 Main Street
Malden, MA 02148, USA

ISBN-13: 978-0-7456-5032-6
ISBN-13: 978-0-7456-5033-3(pb)

A catalogue record for this book is available from the British Library.

Typeset in 10.25 on 13 pt FF Scala
by Servis Filmsetting Ltd, Stockport, Cheshire
Printed and bound in Great Britain by the MPG Books Group

For further information on Polity, visit our website: www.politybooks.com

Contents

Figures and Tables

Acknowledgments

Many ideas went into the writing of this book, and my debt to colleagues, current and former students, and friends who shared in their formulation – or merely helped sharpen my thinking – are too numerous to acknowledge completely. Among those whose ideas have been especially illuminating regarding the importance of how we manage and care for water, to questions of justice, community, authority, power, public good, and social learning, have been Helen Ingram, Henry Vaux, Jean-Daniel Saphores, Stan Grant, Joshua Gellers, Maria Carmen Lemos, Dodd Galbreath, Aaron Routhe, Nancy Brannon, and Denise Fort. I am also grateful to two anonymous reviewers, and for the support of the faculty and staff of the School of Social Ecology at the University of California, Irvine. Thanks also go to Louise Knight and David Winters at Polity for the opportunity to contribute to this innovative series. Finally, I dedicate this book to Justin Paul, whose generation will inherit many of the problems chronicled here, but in which I am confident solutions will be found. Last but not least, I also dedicate this book to Jill, without whose love, patience, and encouragement it would not have been possible

Acknowledgments

CHAPTER ONE

Freshwater: Facts, Figures, Conditions

Freshwater is our planet's most precious resource. Every living thing needs it to survive, but in many places people increasingly face difficulty finding it. In Sana'a, the capital of Yemen, some two-thirds of the city's two million residents rely on private water deliveries by teamsters because the region is running out of groundwater. Those who cannot afford to pay queue up at spigots located outside mosques to gather free water when it is available. It is not unusual to see women collecting families' shower water to re-use for laundry.

While international aid agencies have proposed reducing rural groundwater mining, building additional wells, and restricting agricultural irrigation, no one seems to think these remedies will be enough to help Sana'a. Some believe the underlying problem is a lack of rain made worse by climate change. Others point to continued in-migration from the country's poor, drought-stricken rural areas – to the tune of 150,000 people a year. Some things are certain: the city cannot afford additional water mains; most of Yemen's aquifers are drying up; and the government has been battling Shiite Muslim rebels in the north, a separatist movement in the south, a resurgent Al Qaeda movement, and piracy in the Gulf of Aden. In short, any remedies to its water shortage must reckon with Yemen's violence, instability, and poverty.[1]

If too little freshwater is Yemen's problem, how to pay for it is never far from the minds of most Bolivians. In 1997, in order to receive a World Bank loan, the country's congress

voted to turn over control of its water utilities to two corporations – one, French and the other, American. Both imposed
strict rules on urban residents' ability to collect rainwater
from their roofs, imposed charges for drawing water from private wells, and increased service rates by nearly 200 percent.

Responses to these actions were swift. Uprisings occurred
in Cochabamba and La Paz as poor, angry residents protested
these actions, and martial law was imposed in an effort to
restore order. Bechtel and Aguas de Illimani SA (a subsidiary
of France's Suez), the companies granted licenses to operate
Bolivia's utilities, countered that higher rates were necessary
to expand service and compensate for previous government
corruption that had squandered resources which could have
been used to improve water delivery and treatment infrastructure. Their defense was to no avail. Both companies
abandoned their operations and, in 2005, President Evo
Morales established a Ministry of Water and charged it with
overseeing public supply and providing universal access. The
country's constitution now guarantees a right to water and
bans privatization. Despite reform, provision remains woe-
fully inadequate because the country is too poor to invest in
reliable freshwater supplies or better treatment. In 2008, the
government appropriated a mere $800,000 for nationwide
improvements.[2]

While talk in many parts of the world focuses on the possibility of "water wars" prompted by shortages and exorbitant
cost, in other places too much water is the problem. In the past
decade, South Asia, China, and the American Middle West
and South have endured severe floods that have destroyed
homes and farms and forced people to flee from rising waters.
We know floods occur naturally, and that human folly sometimes worsens its effects (as, for example, when people choose
to live in floodplains or low-lying coastal zones prone to storm
surges). However, politics sometimes intrudes to worsen its

impact in other ways. For instance, at the height of the cata-strophic Indus River basin floods in Pakistan in 2010, wealthy landowners in southern Sindh province dynamited dikes to protect their flood-threatened properties. Levee systems were breached at junctures where wheat, rice, and cotton were cul-tivated by poorer villagers, powerless to oppose their wealthy neighbors' heavily armed militias. Breeching the levees not only worsened a natural disaster, but ensured that its impacts fell most heavily on those least able to recover.[3]

Other freshwater problems are chronicled daily. In Hungary in 2010, a ruptured tailings dam from a poorly man-aged chemical plant unleashed millions of gallons of heavy metals and other contaminants into local rivers – threatening drinking water and contaminating farms. In Ethiopia, mean-while, thousands of villagers eagerly await completion of a massive dam, Gilgel Gibe III, that promises cheap electricity and water for irrigating staple crops. Downstream, however, some Kenyans fear the project may impede river flows that support their fisheries and farms.[4]

Are these problems isolated incidents, or do they point to a global crisis? This book contends that they are *inter-connected* threats to our livelihoods and welfare. What links them is the concept of *sustainability*: ensuring that the various ways we manage freshwater for growing food and fiber, producing energy, making and transporting goods, and meeting house-hold needs do not impair the welfare of other living things, or of future generations. Sustainability also means promot-ing development, protecting the environment, and advancing justice. Yet the way freshwater is managed often does just the opposite. Moreover, when we abuse *other* resources that interact with water we create unsustainable conditions for freshwater management in two ways.

First, any actions that exhaust, deplete, degrade, or pollute water adversely affect both nature *and* people. Once a dam is built, it alters a stream's flow and its surrounding physical and social environment. Similarly, when a river is diverted from its course to slake a city's thirst, the region in which the river's course was changed may find its economy and politics forever changed. Second, many actions designed to avert floods or drought, protect or restore water quality, or provide additional freshwater often fail to account for a society's ability to achieve these objectives fairly, and without unjustly burdening certain groups.

The aim of this book is two-fold: to convey the magnitude of these underlying threats to freshwater sustainability, and to suggest how they might be prevented. We examine "big" threats such as the plight of refugees and the building of huge dams, as well as less dramatic but no less serious ones, such as pollution and the loss of biodiversity. We also examine who controls freshwater, whether growing private control of water supplies is good or bad, and if what we pay for freshwater is fair. We further discuss alternative ways of providing fresh-water, including desalination and wastewater recycling, and whether they can equitably slake our planet's thirst. Finally, we reflect on whether access to freshwater can be thought of as a basic human *right:* there is certainly no debate that it is a fundamental human *need.*

Four principles guide our analysis. First, the world's fresh-water is unevenly distributed *and* unequally used. Growing demands and factors such as climate change will likely worsen this unevenness and inequality. Second, threats to freshwater quality continue to diminish its usability and endanger public health. Third, competition over freshwater is growing because it is a resource increasingly subject to trans-boundary dispute, and increasingly an object of global trade. Finally, when demands for water exceed availability in a given locale, stress and conflict arise, including over proposed methods to make additional water available.

Overview of Global Freshwater

Freshwater is naturally rare. This fact may, at first glance, seem surprising. As shown in figure 1.1, although two-thirds of the earth's surface is covered by water, most of it is salt water found in oceans. Freshwater comprises some 3 percent of the total, and a large proportion of this is unavailable for use because it is frozen in ice caps and glaciers or locked away as soil moisture.

Freshwater is also geographically unevenly distributed. While many Asian, African, and Middle Eastern countries lack abundant freshwater, so does much of Europe (see figure 1.2). The unevenness is caused by climate (which affects precipitation, evaporation, and stream flow), and by geography and geology, including the movement of water under and on the earth's surface, all of which helps determine when, as well as where, it will be made available.

How we use freshwater is also highly variable, both by sector and region. Production of food and fiber currently account for some 70 percent of global water use. Freshwater use closely tracks production of these goods. From 1900 to 2000, global water demands rose six-fold, more than twice the rate of population growth. This is primarily due to agriculture, with urban or municipal use a distant second (figure 1.3). As discussed in chapters 2 and 3, this massive use of freshwater by agriculture

97.2% = saltwater in oceans
2.14% = ice caps and glaciers
0.61% = groundwater
0.009% = surface water
0.0005% = soil moisture
Source: US Geological Survey

Figure 1.1 Distribution of global freshwater

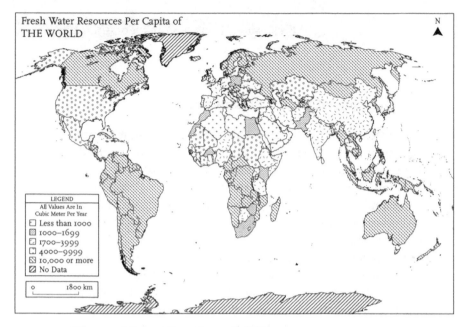

Figure 1.2 Per capita water availability

Estimated annual world water use
km³ per year

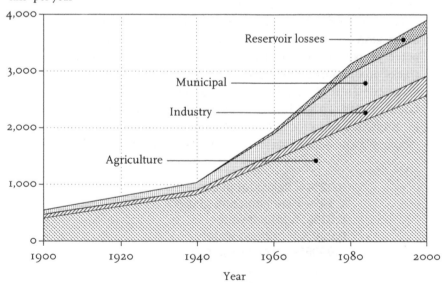

Figure 1.3 Global freshwater uses

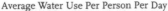

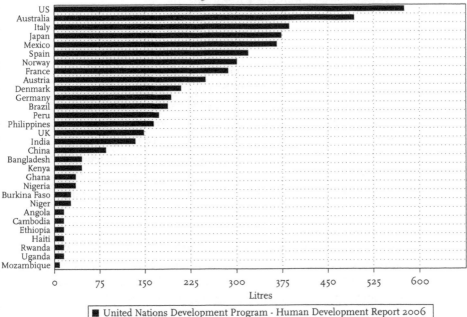

■ United Nations Development Program - Human Development Report 2006

Figure 1.4 Per capita water uses by country

poses a number of challenges due to growing competition from cities and other large user sectors (e.g., energy). It also creates numerous water quality problems, including pesticide and fertilizer runoff, as we discuss in the next section.

In comparing per capita freshwater usage by *country* (figure 1.4), a striking fact is that, irrespective of its availability, people in developed countries use comparatively large amounts of water – up to 10 times as much per person – compared to those in the poorest nations. While affluence explains some of this, specific water uses (e.g., agriculture, energy production) are also important. When we combine the uneven distribution of water on the one hand, with the amounts needed for irrigation of crops and by people living in water-poor regions on the other, we can appreciate how scarcity and adverse quality threatens food supply and human health. We can also understand growing calls for global marketing of freshwater.

For example, Canada, a nation of 33 million, possesses some

20 percent of the world's potable freshwater. Meanwhile, other countries, particularly in the populous and rapidly growing Middle East, are nearly bereft of sufficient freshwater for the needs of their growing populations. Because Canada is potentially a net exporter of water, prospects for developing lucrative exchanges with other countries have been discussed. These opportunities are beginning to arouse awareness of the sustainability problems such trades might generate, as we discuss in chapter 4.[5]

In countries that are short of water, a different set of responses is arising – fear regarding the security of freshwater supplies is giving rise to efforts to impound greater quantities of freshwater behind massive dams. The goal is to avert shortages, propel industrial development through cheap hydropower, and provide irrigation and flood control to ensure higher rates of food production. Such efforts are taking place in a number of rapidly developing countries, as we will see in chapters 2 and 3, most notably in China, India, Brazil, and Ethiopia.

There is growing consensus among scientists that climate change poses an unprecedented threat to the availability and quality of freshwater. In chapter 2, we more fully examine the implications of this threat for freshwater quality, supply, and use. Here, we briefly discuss some of its implications for availability. In the 1980s, climate scientists' models indicated that changes in patterns and amounts of precipitation might become important consequences of climate change. Growing evidence, constantly being re-evaluated by scientists from the UN's Intergovernmental Panel on Climate Change, US Global Change Research Program, and other organizations, point to worsening conditions occurring sooner than previously expected, especially at the extremes of water availability. Stated simply, areas already experiencing periodic drought or flood are likely to see worse drought and flooding in the future, while uneven patterns of precipitation are likely to become even more extreme.

Despite ongoing debates regarding the evidence for climate change, among those who study water there is a growing conviction that a changing climate is already affecting precipitation – or lack of it. Floods that previously had a probability of 1-in-100 years now appear to be more frequent in some areas – South Asia being one of them. In addition, snowpack – the dominant source of freshwater for the Western US and other regions – is lower in volume and, on average, melts earlier in the spring. This affects farmers (who must plan irrigation schedules accordingly) as well as water utility planners (who will have to anticipate potential decreases of supply in summer).

No summary account can do justice to the magnitude of the changes being forecast. Nevertheless, the following are generally thought to encompass those already occurring: increased drought in mid-latitudes; mountain glaciers melting at unprecedented rates on every continent; earlier vegetation blooms in the spring and summer – with photosynthesis occurring longer during the fall; snow and ice cover decreasing in size and melting earlier, while total annual snowfall amounts in far northern latitudes increase; and, curiously, more water availability in the moist tropics and in higher latitudes (see figure 1.5).[6]

What all of this means remains anyone's guess, but it appears certain that, together with the uneven availability of freshwater in many parts of the world, and its rising cost, climate change can only make matters worse. For example, Sana'a may become the world's first capital city to run out of drinking water by 2025. And even if climate change alone is not the cause of Sana'a's problems, it is likely a contributing factor. Similarly, while no one can say for certain that the recent Indus floods in Pakistan were caused by climate

- Changes in the seasonal distribution and amount of precipitation.
- An increase in precipitation intensity under most situations.
- Changes in the balance between snow and rain.
- Increased evapo-transpiration and a reduction in soil moisture.
- Changes in vegetation cover resulting from changes in temperature and precipitation.
- Consequent changes in management of land resources.
- Accelerated melting of glacial ice.
- Increases in fire risk in many areas.
- Increased coastal inundation and wetland loss from sea level rise.
- Effects of CO_2 on plant physiology, leading to reduced transpiration and increased water use efficiency.

Source: Climate Institute, 2010. http://www.climate.org/topics/water.html

Figure 1.5 Effects of climate change on the freshwater cycle

change, we do know that floods in this region are likely to increase in magnitude if glacial melting in the Himalayas worsens (as climatologists forecast). Thus, we would not be surprised if more levee-busting efforts, like the example discussed earlier, were to occur – worsening the plight of that country's rural poor.

Water Quality, Health, and Environment

Threats to freshwater quality – unlike freshwater availability – are almost solely the result of human activity. Pollution of waterways and groundwater is caused by discharges of sewage from industry, as well as treated and untreated human and animal wastes. In addition to these "point-source" discharges, so-called because they are attributable to a single pipe or point-of-origin, such as a water treatment plant, factory, or power plant – and can often be treated at their source – is non-point "runoff." The latter cannot be attributed to a single point-of-origin, and is much harder to prevent. Non-point pollution flows off of paved and unpaved urban surfaces, as well as farms and eroded and denuded lands (i.e., those that have experienced clear-cutting of forests or unregulated grazing of livestock). It then finds its way into streams, lakes, ponds, and estuaries.

Both sources of pollution contain various toxic chemicals, as well as bacteria and even viruses. Non-point pollution is particularly vexing because it contains a wide range of hazardous substances ranging from oils, fertilizers, pesticides, and even soil and sediments. The latter not only choke fish, but provide a solid surface for various other contaminants to adhere to, making these persistent threats to people and the environment.

Worldwide, water quality has in some respects actually improved since the 1970s as a result of aggressive efforts to reduce point-source discharges into rivers, streams, lakes, estuaries, and aquifers. These improvements have been achieved thanks largely to explicit pollution standards and strictly enforced regulations first established in the US and other industrialized nations. These have been implemented through a wide range of tools such as discharge permits, effluent fees, and pollution taxes. Despite this success, concerns over the impact of polluted water on public health continue to grow because less developed countries are not making nearly as much progress in utilizing these tools to alleviate the impacts of point-source discharges, and because runoff pollution, which is much harder to regulate and control, may be worsening in both developed and developing countries.

There are many reasons for this developing country lag in addressing water pollution. Weak regulation of industry, coupled with untreated sewage and lack of funding for adequate treatment systems, are major culprits. Others include the lack of sound city planning and zoning regulations to control industrial and housing developments, made worse by persistent poverty and the inferior status of local government in developing countries.[7]

Water pollution ranks among the world's most urgent public health problems. This is illustrated by a number of alarming statistics furnished by the United Nations and its affiliated organizations. Currently, some 2.6 billion people worldwide lack access to a simple improved latrine system, and an estimated 1.1 billion have no access to improved drinking water sources. As a result, 1.6 million die annually from diarrheal diseases (e.g., cholera) due to lack of access to safe drinking water as well as basic sanitation – 90 percent of its victims are children under five.

Estimates project that 7 billion people in half the world's nations face shortages of potable water by 2050. In addition, some 160 million people are currently infected with schistosomiasis, causing tens of thousands of deaths yearly, while 500 million people are at risk of trachoma, from which 146 million are threatened by blindness, while 6 million are visually impaired. Intestinal diseases plague the developing world due to inadequate drinking water, sanitation, and hygiene; 133 million suffer from high intensity intestinal infections; and there are approximately 1.5 million cases of clinical hepatitis each year. We explore what can be done about this threat to sustainable freshwater in chapter 2.

In recent years, the emergence of newer and especially challenging polluting activities hold the potential for unleashing even greater, but preventable, risks to aquatic life and human health and well-being. These activities conjure "what if" scenarios – what would happen if these activities were to spin out of control? Two examples are oil and tar sands development, a potential threat to surface water quality, and surface and groundwater contamination from pharmaceutical and personal care products – or PPCPs.

For over 40 years, Syncrude, Canada's largest oil producer, has been working to extract oil from bitumen-laced tar sands in Alberta along the Athabasca River, a tributary of the Mackenzie, western Canada's largest river. Some 750,000 barrels of oil per day are "mined" through a combination of steam injection and caustic chemical mixing in a complex process that extracts crude oil from the sands and transports it to refineries in Edmonton and the US. The adverse environmental impacts of this process are enormous, ranging from deforestation; the removal of soil and peat overlying the sands; the diversion of freshwater to produce the oil (it takes three barrels of water converted to steam to extract a barrel of petroleum); discharges into the river from the heating plants that extract the oil; and the discharge of mine tailings into ponds adjacent to the Athabasca River.

If the dikes holding back this contaminated sludge failed, enormous plumes of wastes would be dumped into the river, devastating fisheries that some 20,000 tribal nation members – called "First Citizens" – depend on for their livelihoods. One threat has already been implicated by tar sands development: the leakage of some 45,000 gallons per day of sludge from an older containment pond whose tailings may be responsible for elevated contaminant levels in fish, and additional environmental and public health problems in the region.

Most Albertans oppose further tar sands development until its existing impacts are mitigated and their re-occurrence prevented. However, US support for Canadian oil exports (the former receives some 19 percent of its oil from Canada, and half of that from Alberta tar sands) remains high. The oil sands industry – and the risks to water quality it poses – will persist for the foreseeable future, or until an environmental calamity occurs.[8] The case exemplifies the challenges in protecting freshwater quality when contending values for energy development, economic growth, environmental protection, and the rights of indigenous peoples clash. We take up this value clash in chapters 3 and 5.

PPCPs embrace a wide array of products and activities, including prescription and over-the-counter therapeutic drugs; veterinary medications; fragrances, cosmetics, and sun-screen products; medical laboratory diagnostic agents; vitamins; caffeine; and runoff from so-called Concentrated Animal Feeding Operations, or CAFOs – a growing industry in many parts of the world where livestock is raised for high-profit commercial sale. Traces of PPCPs have shown up in public water supplies worldwide. Even in barely detectable amounts, they can disrupt endocrine systems in people and fish; cause human fetal exposures at low levels; and generate other long-term health effects. Moreover, they accumulate over time, may be passed down through generations, and enter freshwater supplies through many sources.

Sampling in the US alone has found 95 common compounds, one-third of which are unregulated antibiotic and anti-bacterial compounds that defy conventional treatment. An array of agencies recommend four remedies: long-term monitoring of PPCP accumulation in water supplies; introducing expensive technology to remove PPCPs (such as more intensive chlorination, filtering through granulated carbon and ultra-violet light – the former may actually create hazardous disinfection by-products); adopting voluntary disposal measures to avoid surface and groundwater contamination (e.g., disposing of PPCPs in trash rather than flushing them down sinks or toilets); and community "take back" programs. Reliance on greater public education to avoid careless exposure remains a key strategy.[9]

Tar sands development, PPCP pollution, and similar threats prompt us to realize that water quality problems cannot be reduced to simplistic distinctions between developing and developed countries. Wealthier countries can better afford to treat their drinking water, and have been relatively more successful in reducing the health and environmental risks from some pollutants. However, the lifestyles many developed countries have promoted – affluence fueled by carbon-based energy, and made pain-free by pharmaceuticals and beautified by cosmetics – threaten sustainable freshwater management by posing new dangers to water quality.

Globalization and Competition

Drainage basins and aquifers (underground pockets that contain freshwater from rain and snowmelt) flow from higher to lower elevations, and in doing so, they ignore political boundaries. Thus, decisions over freshwater management made in one part of a basin often affect users in another, while people in different parts of a basin may differ in *how* they make primary use of freshwater. This is what we mean by freshwater competition.

For instance, in the Western US, the same Colorado River that irrigates farms in Wyoming and Colorado quenches the thirst of Phoenix, Los Angeles, and Boulder City, Nevada. The same river, impounded by Hoover and Glen Canyon Dams to avert floods and irrigate farms in California's Imperial Valley, also furnishes electricity for the neon lights of Las Vegas and for air conditioners in Tucson, Arizona. These contending uses may conflict with one another, especially during periods of acute drought or major floods, and this has given rise to various schemes to harness freshwater to benefit *different* users – as we discuss in chapters 3 and 4.

Competition over the same sources of freshwater is not a new problem. It is as old as civilization. Some historians suggest that the struggle to harness freshwater was central to the development of the first nation-states, including the political systems of Egypt, India, China, Mesopotamia, Rome, and Pre-Columbian societies. In furnishing both irrigation and urban supply, many ancient societies relied upon tightly organized, authoritarian systems of control that often employed slave labor or other indentured servitude to build, maintain, and operate large-scale water delivery systems. These societies' rulers were, in effect, directors of elaborate networks of hydraulic works designed to provide ample food supplies and ensure potable water. The public works that resulted from these efforts, many of which remain in use today, are testimony to their enduring success. And, comparable forms of control arose in modern societies through privately advocated, government subsidized reclamation and flood control projects, as in the American West (chapter 3).[10]

Ancient societies also cooperated with neighbors to ascertain the proper boundaries of watersheds, and to conjointly manage waters flowing across their common territories. As long ago as 3000 years BC, for example, several Mesopotamian city-states concluded treaties in an effort to quell frequent conflicts over water supplies and their ownership.[11] What makes our era's preoccupations different are that: competition over freshwater is becoming more acute, particularly across national boundaries; and freshwater is becoming viewed as a global commodity, bought and sold like other natural resources such as timber or oil.

Trans-boundary sharing of freshwater generates a host of competitive pressures that are increasingly difficult to amicably resolve. In recent years, Mexico and the US, for example, have debated how to define extraordinary drought, allocate water during shortages, and cooperatively prepare for climate extremes affecting the Colorado and Rio Grande Rivers. Both rivers originate in the US and flow *towards* Mexico. A series of agreements, including a 1906 Rio Grande Convention and 1944 US–Mexico Treaty (the latter established an International Boundary Water Commission) contain specific clauses related to "extraordinary droughts." Both treaties require the US government to apprise Mexico of the onset of drought conditions, and to adjust water deliveries to Mexican customers accordingly.[12]

In recent years, improvements in long-range weather forecasting, greater understanding of climate, and closer monitoring of water withdrawals have made it possible for both nations to more precisely calculate threats to stream flow and to share information. However, these same factors worsen cross-border problems. Both countries are reluctant to negotiate to re-open these agreements for fear they may lead to reduced allocations or alterations of water rights.

Africa's Nile basin illustrates a comparable set of challenges in a multinational context. Ten countries – Kenya, Burundi, Rwanda, Tanzania, Eritrea, Ethiopia, Sudan, Egypt, the Democratic Republic of Congo, and Uganda – share the Nile River. Since 1998, these countries have been negotiating a new framework agreement because of frustration with the previous one: Currently, negotiations on this Nile Basin Initiative – to revisit how freshwater should be allocated to some 160 million people in a 3.1 million km^2 region – are at a stalemate, because Egypt and Sudan, downstream countries with the largest populations, refuse to relinquish power to upstream countries over withdrawals.

It is unusual for downstream users to have greater control over rivers than those living upstream, where a river begins. This exceptional case results from a 1929 British decision that granted legal rights to a fixed amount of Nile water to Egypt and Sudan – then the most populous countries in the basin. This practice gradually evolved into a formal agreement which now permits both countries to draw 74 billion gallons per year from the river. Ethiopia is fiercely opposed to continuing this practice. Sitting astride the Blue Nile, a major tributary, Ethiopia recently built a hydroelectric dam without Egypt's permission, creating additional friction that may impede a new agreement to share water.

Meanwhile, Lake Victoria, a major source of the Nile, is falling some 2.5 meters every three years – likely due to climate change, experts contend – while the basin's population is projected to double between now and 2035. Chronic drought and the siphoning off of upstream flows are also taxing Nile Delta rice farmers in Egypt who have been ordered to conserve water by planting fewer acres – despite the nation's need for additional food.

At a 2009 Council of Ministers meeting in Egypt, Henriette Ndombe, Executive Director of the Initiative, urged participants to "devise feasible options/proposals for the finalization of the Cooperative Framework Agreement," and appealed to basin countries to "move forward in the spirit of cooperation on the basis of One Nile, One Basin, and One Vision." While an explicit goal of this agreement is permitting use of the Nile "sustainably and effectively towards development," a settlement along these lines remains far from certain.[13]

Economic globalization increasingly knits together products dependent on water (e.g., food, fiber, and fuels), thereby converting freshwater itself into a tradable commodity – and in ways that reach far beyond the borders of a single country. The capacity to buy and sell freshwater, and the commodities whose production depends on it, complicate control, accountability, and fairness by potentially placing power over freshwater in the hands of large multinational corporations.

We examine this issue in detail in chapters 4 and 5. At this juncture it is important to note how this issue is a factor in disputes we have already discussed.

For example, the Bolivian case illustrates how globalization raises apprehensions over water security and the equity of decisions in two ways. First, while public protests eventually forced Bechtel to abandon its water operations in the provincial center of Cochabamba and for Aguas de Illimani SA to do the same in La Paz, the issues giving rise to these disputes remain trenchant. In both communities, local citizens were virtually excluded from decisions regarding freshwater allocation, cost, and access. Vital decisions were relinquished by the central government to privately owned utilities accountable to stockholders and not responsive to, or very accommodating towards, the needs of local citizens. Second, the Bolivian case strongly suggests that those who manage freshwater – whether public or private entities (see chapter 4) – must account for the interests and needs of those who use it. The average person's welfare in regards to freshwater, and the right to participate in decisions over its use, are morally important. Excluding people from these decisions is likely to lead to strident resistance.

Finally, globalization also exploits the unevenness of freshwater availability previously discussed, as well as the unequal uses to which freshwater is subject. International trade is leading to a growing recognition of the importance of what some are coming to call *virtual water*: any water-intensive product (e.g., food, energy) heavily traded over large distances between importing and exporting countries. By some estimates, the total global volume of virtual water flows in commodities is 1,625 billion m^3 per year, or about 40 percent of total annual worldwide water consumption.[14]

As an outcome of globalization, virtual water may make the disposition of the world's freshwater more inequitable

and insecure by moving water in the form of crops and industrial products from countries with low water productivity to
those whose productivity is higher. Such economic changes
would put additional pressure on local supplies, and force
the transformation of local economies in ways that may not
be beneficial to developing countries seeking to become economically more self-sufficient.

In short, while both competition and cooperation over
freshwater result from the fact that watersheds do not respect
political boundaries, the global context in which both take
place is radically changing. Climate change, demands for
greater participation, and calls for fairer allocation of trans-
boundary water are forcing previous management practices
to change. Hydraulic societies, once governed by elites who
could harness and allocate however they wanted, no longer
exist. And mandates bestowed by former empires no longer
hold sway – as the upper Nile basin states' rejection of British
rules of allocation illustrates. In short, sharing of freshwater
now occurs in a framework of new political, economic, legal,
cultural, ethical, and environmental demands – including
another threat: water stress.

Stress: Growing Demand, Dwindling Supply

Stress is an imbalance between available supplies within various regions on one hand, and demands on those supplies by
multiple users on the other. Most commonly linked to population growth, extreme drought, and inadequately maintained
or deteriorating infrastructure, the causes of stress include
a combination of demographics, climate, and econom-
ics. Understanding stress is vitally important for discerning
the localized pressures of climate change, mass migration,
agricultural production, and even energy use on freshwater –
issues we discuss in chapters 2 and 3. One arena where water

stress is most vivid is so-called "megacities" – urban areas composed of tens of millions of people. Megacities are global "flashpoints" for the types of conflicts over freshwater we are likely to see more frequently in the future.[15] They are also a touchstone for innovations in conservation, wastewater re-use and recycling, and desalination (chapter 5).

Megacities contribute to water stress in three major ways. First, they are often located some distance from the water sources needed to maintain their growth; thus they must divert water from outlying rural areas which, in turn, often produce the food and fiber to support them. Second, megacities' soaring birth rates and in-migration place extra burdens upon antiquated water infrastructure, and generate severe health and hygiene problems. Third, cities generally, and megacities in particular, generate huge volumes of wastewater which are costly to treat and, if left untreated, contaminate local wells and streams. They also impose a huge *spatial* "footprint" on their region through sprawling horizontal urban development and annexation of some outlying districts – contributing to greater runoff pollution, diminished groundwater recharge, and a higher likelihood of distribution system leaks and other failures.

Mexico City, Mumbai, India, and Lagos, Nigeria exemplify some of these challenges and their management. Mexico City is one of the world's most rapidly growing urban centers with over 21 million people. Some 70 percent of its water comes from groundwater reserves first tapped by the Aztecs. Over-drafting of these reserves is forcing the city to seek alternative sources in its outlying region, including deep wells in the Lerma Valley, diverting water from the Cuztamala and Amacuzac Rivers to decrease reliance on groundwater, and reusing wastewater and capturing and storing rainwater. Some three-quarters of urban wastewater is re-used for irrigation, but very little is treated and re-used for residential consumption.

Like Mexico City, Mumbai also imports freshwater portions from its outlying region. This practice has generated conflict with rural districts that resent diversion from rural areas to meet Mumbai's demands, especially since those plans are supported by state, national, and even international aid agencies. Plans for new infrastructure have been devised, including linking the city to more distant parts of the Vaitarna and Ulhas River basins to create one of the largest and most technically complex water supply systems in the world.

Lagos has ample surface and underground water resources, and thus does not have to divert water supplies great distances as does Mumbai (which diverts water from no fewer than six sources) and Mexico City. However, like Mumbai, Lagos increasingly relies upon ad hoc sources of freshwater. Many households are not connected to existing piped water systems from which precise flow measurements can be derived; and those who are connected do not necessarily rely on piped water for all their domestic needs – rainwater harvesting is a major freshwater source. Thousands of businesses and residential neighborhoods collect and store rainwater, a resourceful undertaking during periodic dry spells. Groundwater is also provided through hundreds of boreholes and illegal wells, and private tankers serve as a third "tier" provider in both Lagos and Mumbai – supplementing official supplies and illegal taps and other sources.

Finally, all three cities suffer from inadequate potable supply. Inequalities mark everyday life, and are reflected by uneven access to potable water – poorer residents are routinely shooed away from taps – which prompts many of the extra-legal water acquisition efforts. Ironically, such injustices are also more common in rural areas, and spur new waves of migration to these cities.

Just as stress worsens regional conflict over freshwater, proposed methods to make additional water available to cities and their outlying regions also generate conflict. Several options are being considered and in some instances adopted to provide additional freshwater to meet the world's teeming demands, including tiered or conservation pricing, metering, desalination, and wastewater recycling. We discuss these options in chapters 4 and 5. At this juncture, it is worth noting that conflict between large cities and their outlying regions, as well as the proclivity to innovate in response to regional stress, is nothing new. A hopeful trend is that large cities have been doing this for quite some time.

For example, Tokyo's rapid economic progress following World War II demanded dramatic alterations in water supply to match its growth. Urbanization and economic development increased water demands for domestic and industrial uses. By the late 1970s, growing water consumption led to a distorted imbalance within Tokyo's water system. Rapid urbanization led to smaller rivers and waterways being covered by concrete and pavement in order to create new space – and to abate urban flooding, a serious problem. Meanwhile increased freshwater consumption led to declines in groundwater levels, poor river water quality, and land subsidence. To acquire additional water necessary to meet demands, the city has begun employing a combination of regulation, technology, and citizen participation efforts. Rainwater harvesting for miscellaneous use has been employed on a widespread individual residential scale. Viewed as a source of water supply, rainwater harvesting practices are applauded as practical means to make citizens better aware of the need for sustainable water use.

Reclaimed wastewater is also being introduced to restore the vitality of streams. Wastewater is seen as a resource for landscape irrigation and environmental purposes – it increases water supplies by also reducing the demand for higher quality, more expensively treated water. Use of reclaimed wastewater also reduces further accumulation of polluted water and discharge. This practice is also viewed as economically efficient because it is cheaper than transporting water from distant sources. Tokyo has coupled these approaches with the implementation of withdrawal restrictions on groundwater.

Two US metropolises that divert water from distant sources – New York and Los Angeles – may have much to teach other megacities regarding stress and how to cope with it. Early in their histories these cities, in their quest to acquire water, adopted a hegemonic relationship with their neighbors. In effect, they sought to control regional sources that could satisfy current as well as projected water needs. They also faced many of the same challenges to public health and wastewater management that their developing nation counterparts face today, including managing foul and unhealthful water and preventing the spread of infectious, waterborne disease; deciding on an appropriate role for private versus public sector investment to improve infrastructure and secure reliable supplies; and how to compensate for the adverse environmental and economic impacts imposed on their outlying regions through their efforts to divert water from them. These efforts, we now know, led to an unsustainable system for regional freshwater stewardship.

Over time, and under external pressure, both cities embraced collaboration with adjacent communities to address water supply and quality issues, whose scope and impact required regional accommodation and sharing of authority. They also embraced conservation and other measures to better use the freshwater available to them without imposing continued stress on their outlying regions.

In sum, many of the world's large cities are seeking innovative ways to meet water demands. Although they have made strides in locating new sources and managing demands, these remedies remain temporary expedients. Drawing water from distant locations perpetuates unsustainable uses. However, while technological innovations provide an array of opportunities to quench a city's water needs, they also pose their own equity challenges including where and when these technologies should be introduced; who should pay for them; and whether their risks are acceptable. We take up these issues in chapter 5.

Going Forward

Will there be enough – and clean enough – freshwater to support the world's growing population? Can we manage freshwater sensibly and prudently, and with proper regard for the welfare of future generations? And, will its management become increasingly privatized: a trend that accelerated in developing countries in the 1990s, when criticisms over costs, benefits, and access to clean water became foci of struggles over sustainable development, public participation in decisions, and social justice? While we will attempt to answer these complex and provocative questions, it must be appreciated that the reader is not being drawn into a mere academic debate. These are urgent questions with uncertain and, at best, sometimes contradictory answers with incalculable significance for people and politics. For example, we may be able to have an adequate supply of freshwater for all necessary uses, but it may not be "free" or inexpensive. Moreover, a "growing" population, in both numbers and affluence, may be able to depend on an adequate supply of freshwater if we take proper measures to conserve its use. However, "adequate" is not the same as "profligate." The wasteful uses of water to which many of us in the West have become accustomed may have become a thing of the past – and probably should.

A 2009 report by the Council on Hemispheric Affairs contends there has been "severe mismanagement in water and sanitation, which will be exponentially exacerbated in coming decades by population growth combined with declining resources" – a charge which squarely places blame for these problems on failures of politics. Moreover, the report suggests, the decisions that will determine whether we can effectively meet this management challenge cannot wait for future generations to answer – it is our job to begin to solve these problems now, before it is too late to avert possible catastrophe. In each subsequent chapter, we emphasize the importance of decisions over freshwater as key to alleviating this crisis, and we employ these same four themes to illuminate the challenges: uneven distribution and unequal use, threats to quality, competition among users, and stress within regions.

Chapter 2 discusses the most significant threats to freshwater sustainability, ranging from environmental alteration by farming and energy use to migration. We examine proposals to alleviate shortages, improve quality, reduce stress, and account for uneven distribution through structural measures (e.g., building dams) and through more adaptive measures which rely on the building of social capacity to manage demands and exercise stewardship over regional water resources. A key solution, we suggest, may lie in better use of so-called "social-ecological systems" – ad hoc arrangements that encourage informal collaboration among various protagonists in a given region.

Chapter 3 explores the wide array of human actions that degrade, deplete, diminish, and divert rivers, streams, lakes, and aquifers worldwide. These actions affect not only the quality and quantity of water available to society, but they influence water rights, public health and welfare, and social justice. A range of cases – from the Rhine basin in Europe to the Mississippi basin in the US – illustrate the severe, if often "invisible" challenges posed by these persistent problems to water quality, distribution, competition among users, and stress. Discussion of some very large water projects (China's Three Gorges Dam and Brazil's Itaipu) will show how efforts to solve these problems often generate unanticipated consequences.

Chapter 4 examines the divergent ways water is allocated, regulated, and managed by public and private sector institutions (i.e., public utilities and markets). We consider whether growing corporate provision of water supplies, particularly in developing countries, will lead to more sustainable management, or less, and whether what people are asked to pay for water results in a more efficient, equitable, and publically acceptable way of serving the needs of people and the environment. We also examine the impact of the buying, selling, and leasing of water rights; the transformation of freshwater into a consumer item (i.e., bottled water); and the social unrest generated by efforts to apply capitalist business models of efficiency, profit, and investor return to water provision. We consider the extent to which water management worldwide is becoming a "hybrid" model that seeks to balance stewardship, efficiency, and public accountability – and whether this balance can be achieved.

Finally, chapter 5 seeks to answer the question: How can these critical challenges to water sustainability be solved? Experts and policy makers agree that growing scarcity and the inequality of access to clean, potable freshwater make conflicts more intractable – and that international cooperation will be required to solve these problems. However, amicable and acceptable remedies will only be achieved if cooperation leads to transparent and just agreements to use water, and if decision makers embrace public concerns in proposals for conservation, wastewater re-use, and desalination. We conclude with consideration of the ways in which water is a basic human right, and the extent to which scientists and policy makers are taking seriously calls for a more ethical water policy.

CHAPTER TWO

Geopolitics and Sustainability

Ensuring that the ways we use freshwater to grow food, generate electricity, make and transport goods, and meet household
needs are environmentally safe, economically beneficial, and
socially just is a compelling ideal. It is also an elusive one.
Each time we divert a river from its course, pollute a lake, or
overdraw an aquifer, we risk irreversibly altering the quality
and availability of freshwater for future generations. We also
threaten the long-term survival of other species. Averting such
impacts requires changing our fundamental attitudes toward
water in ways few of us are accustomed to.

Take, for example, *Our Common Future*, a 1983 report written by the UN's "World Commission on Environment and
Development." This report boldly proclaimed that "major,
unintended changes are occurring in the atmosphere, in soils,
in waters, among plants and animals, and in the relationships
among all of these." These changes outrun the capacity of science to fathom their impact, generate adverse consequences,
and inflict threats with which established institutions cannot
cope.[1] What made this report so compelling was that it was
aimed at two different audiences: those living in developed
countries who invest in practices degrading to the environments and freshwater of developing nations, and the
developing countries that allow these practices to take place,
often because they believe they have no choice but to rapidly
exploit their natural resources in order to modernize. In short,
Our Common Future was a plea for us to change our widely

accustomed, antiquated, and short-sighted thinking about freshwater.

An appropriate example that reveals the paradox of freshwater sustainability is the decision by a developing country to dam a river to generate electricity. Such a decision, possibly funded by a developed country hoping to profit from its investment, could force modest peasants to deforest and denude adjacent lands to regain subsistence income lost when formerly arable land was flooded by the dam's construction. In the process, both inundation and, later, deforestation could actually worsen the quality of the local environment while driving the peasants into further debt. Such a paradox is not a hypothetical scenario: Nigeria, Ethiopia, Brazil, China, and other developing countries have experienced it.

Many efforts to try to achieve freshwater sustainability trace their genesis to *Our Common Future*. These efforts have included reports issued by the World Wildlife Fund, International Union on the Conservation of Nature, UN Environment Program, UN Conference on the Environment, UN Sustainability Summit, World Water Forum, and the International Conference on Freshwater, among others. Pressing countries toward lofty aims, their goals included: better provision of potable water and sanitation; more efficiently irrigating crops to ensure that enough food can be grown to satisfy the world's hunger; equitably sharing rivers that traverse the boundaries of two or more countries; empowering local citizens to make some decisions regarding freshwater, independent of their national leaders; delegating authority for planning water and sanitation projects to local governments that are closer to the problems causing degraded quality and diminished supply; and ensuring that rights to freshwater be provided to everyone in a watershed regardless of income, education, gender, or ethnicity. Universally acknowledging that the power of entrenched groups has often led to decisions that too often enrich a few while causing the many to suffer, these efforts prescribed reforms that have engendered broad, but not always *precise*, agreement.

This chapter discusses three significant threats to freshwater sustainability: environmental alteration by agriculture, energy use, and population migration; climate change impacts on practices that degrade water; and, undemocratic and unjust control of freshwater. We examine efforts to alleviate shortages, improve quality, reduce stress, and compensate for the uneven distribution of freshwater through measures ranging from building more dams to less intrusive (and more sustainable) actions that rely instead on building *social capacity*. A key to sustainable freshwater management is adopting a *social-ecological* approach that encourages stakeholders to work together; employs local as well as expert knowledge of the environment; and embraces broad-based participation and inclusion of diverse groups.

An Overview of Threats

Table 2.1 lists seven basic principles of sustainable freshwater management. These criteria are derived from the Pacific Institute, a research foundation that studies the relationship between freshwater use and sustainable development. These principles have the virtue of underscoring the inter-connections between ecological and human health, sound science, and democratic politics in achieving sustainability.

They also underscore a quandary that frequently arises in debates over freshwater sustainability: how do we distinguish between activities that harm freshwater, but may be *reparable* (for example, if polluted waters are cleaned up, if sources of new contamination are averted, and if practices that over-draw groundwater cease?) as opposed to those that *irreversibly alter* freshwater and its capacity to support nature and people? In

Table 2.1	Sustainability criteria for water resources planning[2]
Criteria	**Definition**
Maintaining human health	A basic water requirement will be guaranteed to maintain human health.
Maintaining ecosystem health	A basic water requirement will be guaranteed to maintain and restore the health of ecosystems.
Minimum standards of quality	Water quality will be maintained to meet at least minimum standards. These standards may and will vary depending upon the location of the water, and how the water is to be used.
Long-term freshwater renewability	Human activities will not impair the long-term renewability of freshwater stocks and flows.
Data collection and accessibility	Data and other information on the availability, use, quality, and quantity of water will be collected and made available and accessible to everyone.
Institutional mechanisms for resolving conflict	Institutional mechanisms will be established to prevent, alleviate, and resolve conflicts over water.
Democratic decision making	Water planning and decision making will be democratic, ensuring representation of all affected parties and fostering the direct participation of affected interests.

truth, it is not easy to discern the difference – and sometimes we do not really know until it is too late to do anything. That's the nub of what *Our Common Future* meant when it warned of major, *unintended* changes that could alter freshwater.

Using the seven criteria in table 2.1 as a point of departure, we suggest that irreversible freshwater harms are of two basic types: those affecting freshwater *quantity* and those affecting its *quality*. The first type includes actions that divert water from streams, rivers, and aquifers to such an extent that they reduce stream flow beyond recoverable levels or deplete aquifers beyond their capacity for "recharge" (sometimes called groundwater "mining"). The second type includes activities that contaminate surface- and/or groundwater with chemicals, heavy metals, or pathogens to such a degree that their ability to sustain life is irrevocably tainted, leading to extinction of entire species. Both actions also affect a society's capacity to produce food, energy, and other necessities, leading, in turn, to population dislocation and decisions to divert scarce water supplies from poorer areas (whose populations cannot control or effectively influence these decisions) to wealthier regions – thus affecting social equity as well as the environment. Finally, as we will see, actions that affect quality often also affect quantity – and vice versa. The less water in a stream, the harder it is to dilute pollution, for example.

Three large-scale activities pose potentially irreversible harm to freshwater sustainability. First, across the planet, vast quantities of freshwater are being harvested for agriculture and energy. These *environmental alterations* transform the landscape and, in some cases, ecology, of entire regions. They also generate political conflict between an agriculture sector that is increasingly producing bio-fuels as well as food and fiber, and those who endure the costs of these activities in pollution, greater demands on water supply, and loss of control over its allocation. Ever more migrants from regions where conflict occurs, and who seek sanctuary from violence and famine, are increasingly caught in the middle: inflicting their own pressures on freshwater.[3]

Second, industrial pollution and other practices that degrade water quality and diminish local surface- and groundwater supplies have long plagued the world's most advanced economies. In recent decades, these practices have become copied by many developing countries that seek to rapidly modernize. Worsening this spread of poor freshwater stewardship is the problem of climate change, mentioned in chapter 1. Changes to climate further deplete freshwater, exacerbating poor management practices, and they also worsen water quality. We are beginning to see this trend in places such as Northeast Brazil, sub-Saharan Africa, and parts of the US – among other regions.

Third, those who exercise control over water supply, quality, and allocation – including government agencies, private corporations, and individual landowners who tenaciously hold onto local water rights – are often responsible for faulty, ill-conceived, and unfair decisions regarding freshwater. In recent years, demands that these groups be held more accountable for their decisions have grown. In many countries river basin compacts and other watershed authorities designed to facilitate consensus building and accommodation of divergent interests have been held up as potential models for achieving this goal.[4] As we will see, while these models are germane, they are also difficult to bring about in poor, less developed societies.

Environmental Alterations and Water

Recall from chapter 1 that production of food and fiber account for nearly 70 percent of the world's total freshwater demand. Unlike most uses of water, however, agriculture is what hydrologists call a *consumptive use*. Consumptive uses withdraw water from streams, rivers, other surface water bodies, or aquifers but do not immediately return it to these water bodies in the local vicinity. Instead, the water is literally "consumed" through absorption into plants, crop transpiration, evaporation, or through livestock slaking thirst. Other water uses are also consumptive: we have all seen the plumes of steam rising from power plant cooling towers, for instance. However, these other uses are not as consumptive as agriculture. Moreover, since many forms of agriculture also generate runoff from various chemicals used in destroying pests and fertilizing crops, it is a major source of environmental alteration of freshwater, contributing to potential shortages of local supply and to poor quality.[5] These impacts are becoming more critical for four reasons.

First, population growth in developing countries is escalating demands to produce more food, increasing pressures to consign even more land to cultivating crops. In turn, this is leading to an increase in both the costs and environmental impacts from various "inputs" such as fertilizers and pesticides which farmers are compelled to apply to their lands to ensure high yields and ample profit. Population growth is also encouraging rapid conversion of virgin forests, meadows, and grasslands into cultivated farms and grazing land – further degrading freshwater quality and, in downstream communities, contaminating drinking water, which these communities often cannot afford to treat.

Second, the quest to develop, modernize, and afford rural areas, villages, and cities in developing countries a higher quality of life is adding to demands for additional energy. This is inflicting an unforeseen but dramatic impact on agriculture. Energy demands are expected to grow by some 60 percent over present needs by 2030 in developing countries.[6] While virtually every source of energy depends on water, one rapidly growing energy source in much of the developing world is bio-fuels such as ethanol, which can be produced by converting biomass including trees, grasses, left-over agricultural residue from harvesting crops, and even algae – and then used to heat homes, power motor vehicles, or cook food. Bio-fuels firmly link agriculture and energy production, with dramatic impacts upon freshwater.

The myriad alterations caused by this "energy-water" inter-connection are so critical for understanding the social equity and economic development facets of sustainability as to warrant elaboration. Consider the following: as cropland is diverted from food to energy-crop production, and as developing countries restrict imports of food to *encourage* more domestic farming and greater food security, food prices are likely to rise. We have already seen this occur as the result of corn-based ethanol production in many countries. As food prices rise, the cost of water used for production of *both* food and bio-fuel crops, and to treat the new sources of water supply contamination resulting from this higher production, *also* increases because of demand for additional water.

These costs will be borne mostly by the poorest and least powerful members of society: those who live in rural areas will be forced to produce *more* food, fiber, and bio-fuels to sustain their livelihoods, and to compensate for the higher prices they must pay for potable water. They will also suffer from the impacts to local water quality resulting from these activities. In addition, demands for energy, especially electrical power, in these countries will at least initially be greater in large urban centers as opposed to rural villages. This is likely to lead to greater demands to centralize the management and control of both power production and of the water infrastructure built to supply it, as we will see.

A third agriculture-related impact to freshwater sustainability is mass migration. Water shortages induced by drought, and by excessive groundwater pumping and diversion of rivers and streams to compensate for drought, are producing a mass exodus of subsistence-level pastoralists, peasants, and others who are seeking better economic opportunities elsewhere. The number of refugees driven from their lands through drought, famine, massive flooding, and political violence is difficult to precisely calculate. According to the United Nations, the numbers of *environmentally* displaced people range from 24 million to almost 700 million. Many of these refugees have been forced to relocate or to expediently seek water supplies in neighboring communities close to their own villages, not only because of war, acts of terror against minority groups, or famine, but because of projects designed to relieve regional stress on freshwater.

A good example is the Ganges headwaters region in Northern India, which lies astride the foothills of the Himalayas. Upon completion of the Tehri Dam on the Bhagirathi River, a tributary of the Ganges, and some 200 miles from New Delhi, over 100,000 people had to be relocated. Relocation caused numerous resettlement lawsuits that not only produced local conflict but delayed the dam's completion until the early 2000s. In one instance, a natural spring that fed the nearby village of Pipola dried up, forcing residents to fetch water from wells in a neighboring village, while other villagers simply fled to other neighboring villages to live. In both instances, conflict ensued between older and newer residents over the control and use of local water supplies.[7] This story is becoming more common across India. It belies the fact that a further complication in unraveling connections between migration and water resources is that people rely on the environment for their livelihoods. Policies intended to alleviate poverty and better provide more food and energy (Tehri is a major irrigation project), can also adversely affect political amiability and economic stability through causing large-scale migration. Inundation of arable lands by dams may benefit some, but it can injure others.

Migration also threatens freshwater sustainability by diminishing water quality. Refugees often pass through camps or informal settlements that are artificially, and often briefly, sustained by aid agencies or governments. One result is rapid denuding of the surrounding area as people search for both water and fuel wood in order to survive – leading to deforestation, land clearing, soil degradation, and shortages of clean, potable water. In addition, "migratory pastoralists" – a term applied by anthropologists to peasants and villagers who normally earn their livelihoods through nomadic forms of farming and shepherding – often practice overgrazing of livestock as well as slash and burn agriculture. These activities further impact water quality. And, while migrants are typically rural residents, they increasingly constitute a growing proportion of those seeking better economic opportunities and access to potable water, sanitation services, housing and healthcare, and food stocks in cities. Not surprisingly, these migrants often accelerate the growth of slum communities on the fringes of "megacities." Their presence leads to higher concentrations of water-related public health problems including cholera, dysentery, and other communicable diseases.

As one recent UN report put it: "[the] relation between water and migration is two-way: water stressors drive migration, and migration contributes to water stress."[8] Like the problem of increased agricultural production and its impacts on water, the impact of migration on freshwater sustainability often falls upon the poorest of the poor: those who are displaced not only from their former communities, but from positions of power and influence where they could at least exercise the basic rights of political citizenship.

Finally, while the growth of food, fiber, and bio-fuels production, and the advent of mass migration alter freshwater in unsustainable ways, a less obvious but no less important problem is the growth of *virtual* water use – briefly mentioned in chapter 1. When developing countries seek to become self-sufficient in food, however sensible this option may initially appear, the quest can generate undesirable consequences for water security, especially in arid regions. Food self-sufficiency policies, though beneficial for rural development, increase a country's national water footprint and may forfeit growth in higher income, but less water-intensive sectors. Global virtual water trade could save water, *if* products are traded from countries with high water productivity to countries with lower efficiency. For example, Mexico imports wheat, maize, and sorghum from the US. This requires the US to use 7.1 billion m³ of water a year to produce these grains – a lot of water, certainly. However, if Mexico substituted imports by producing these same crops domestically, it would have to use 15.6 billion m³ of water per year due to differences in climate, soils, and topography. Thus, from a global perspective, trade in cereals saves 8.5 billion m³ of water annually.

Despite some trade from countries with low water productivity to countries with higher productivity, global water savings through international agricultural trade (i.e., virtual water trade) has been estimated at about 350 billion m³ a year, equivalent to 6 percent of the global volume of water used for all agricultural production. Japan, Mexico and most of Europe, the Middle East and North Africa have net virtual water imports. Thus, ensuring food security in many countries strongly depends on having access to external sources of water, or external food supplies.

All these impacts should remind us that, as undesirable as extreme alteration of freshwater by agriculture may be, there is a practical side to this alteration that tempers criticism: it is usually driven by the developing world's unmet needs for economic sustenance. And, the more acute the alteration of freshwater, the more likely it is caused by extreme poverty, material deprivation, and personal insecurity. These problems underscore why sustainable freshwater management remains elusive and paradoxical. Alteration of freshwater and its quality due to food, fiber, energy production, and mass migration results in injustice, further poverty, and greater conflict. At the same time, alteration is caused by the quest to overcome the very same problems.

Climate Change and Sustainability

In chapter 1, we noted how climate change is likely to intensify extreme weather events including droughts, floods, and tropical storms. Less frequently noted by popular commentators are other impacts to freshwater quality and supply. As we have seen, sustainability of freshwater is threatened by pollution and over-allocation. What climate change will do is aggravate these threats possibly to a point of irreversibility. Equally worrisome, assessing the impacts of a changing climate is a daunting challenge: no one is quite certain what the risks are, although they have been better documented in developed countries.

In general, experts agree that six changes are likely (see table 2.2).[9] First, according to the Intergovernmental Panel on Climate Change (IPCC), for the past century or so, while total annual precipitation has actually increased in the northern latitudes, which just happen to be the areas of the globe containing most of the world's developed countries (including the US, with some 4 percent of the world's land area), average precipitation in the developing countries south of the equator has decreased. Regions especially hard hit have been the traditional agricultural and forestry production territories of Africa, Latin America, and South and Southeast Asia.

Coupled with higher temperatures, these changes in precipitation also result in lower soil moisture and substantial reductions in river runoff, trends expected to worsen due to continued warming throughout the twenty-first century. Moreover, to compensate for the effects of drought, withdrawals from streams and reservoirs may increase further, severely degrading stream water quality through lower stream flows, polluted return flows, or both.

Second, climate change can inflict huge economic losses to regionally important economic activities that are dependent

Table 2.2   Major climate impacts to freshwater uses
• Uneven changes in precipitation patterns in northern and southern hemispheres – corresponding to different levels of development.
• Losses in agricultural productivity and urban water supply, especially in already water-stressed regions.
• Warmer surface water temperatures and lower flow volumes worsening impacts of pollution and threatening species.
• Greater flood flow runoff in megacities and worsening of non-point pollution concentrations; play havoc with forestry and crop management.
• Exacerbate pressures on groundwater use, over-drafting, and aquifer depletion.
• Changes in precipitation and stream flow will adversely affect electrical power production availability and distribution system reliability.

on water. For example, an agricultural region may be simultaneously stressed by degraded soil and changes in precipitation caused by climate change, as well as by serious threats to urban water supply. Taking the Southwest US as an example (again, the possible impacts have been better studied there), if the region becomes increasingly arid, as many believe, then warmer temperatures in the future could lead to serious long-term increases in drought, as well as changes to runoff and stream flow, affecting agriculture and urban water supply in cities as diverse in their economic base as Las Vegas, Phoenix, and Los Angeles. Key to understanding these changes for sustainability is the realization that they will not occur in a vacuum, but in a larger context in which water supply is already severely constrained by environmental and economic pressures as well as competition between agricultural needs and those of cities.

Third, we know that industrial and mining activities may irreversibly alter riparian environments within or alongside stream bodies, lakes and estuaries through dumping of mine tailings and toxic pollutants. These practices degrade water quality through depositing contaminants that settle in sediments at the bottom of lakes and streams. By producing warmer surface water temperatures and lower flows, climate change will likely *worsen* the impacts of pollutants through decreases in dissolved oxygen for aquatic species to breathe, and increased flows of polluted runoff, further degrading water quality in receiving lakes, rivers, and streams, especially if these water-bodies carry more nutrients and sediments. This could be just the irreversible "tipping point" needed to threaten extinction to entire aquatic species.

Fourth, in *urbanized* areas – especially large megacities like those we discussed in chapter 1 – increased runoff and flooding can lead to increased amounts of non-point pollutants from landscaped areas, as well as point-source pollutants from the overflow from antiquated or poorly maintained sewer systems. These pose enormous risks to human health through exposure to pesticides and nutrients from adjacent agricultural lands, germs from animal and human wastes, and chemicals from petroleum-based products found on parking lots and commercial properties. We know that such pollutant "shocks" to lakes, rivers, and streams are especially severe if flooding occurs after a prolonged dry spell in which pollutants have accumulated: and such sudden and surprising local weather fluctuations are another symptom of climate change.

IPCC studies also show that natural vegetation cover, integral to a healthy watershed's ability to absorb pollutants, is disturbed by stresses caused by these same surprising weather events, which can occur more often (e.g., die-off during drought, blow-down of trees during tropical storms) and by climate-sensitive disturbances such as pest infestations and wildfire – which some think have been occurring in many boreal forests in Russia, Canada, and elsewhere. Moreover, assuming that knowledge of the impacts of climate change encourages farmers to adjust seasonal decisions regarding cropping patterns, fertilizer use, and increased planting of low water use native plants, these changes in land use will, in turn, further affect water quality and availability. Clearly, connections between land-cover change, runoff, inclement weather, and climate impacts are poorly understood.

Fifth, much of the world depends upon groundwater for its local supply of freshwater, and *groundwater depletion* is already a serious freshwater sustainability problem. Climate change can affect groundwater in myriad and surprising ways. In general, the smaller and more shallow an aquifer, the more changes in precipitation such as those that would be caused by a changing climate would affect groundwater recharge. Moreover, shallow aquifers are usually connected to surface waters which would likely be seriously affected – especially in regions where *conjunctive* water use (the combined withdrawal of surface- and groundwaters that are connected to each other) occurs – as in much of the central plains in the US, the Argentine *pampas*, and the central African *savanna*.

During drought, water tables in unconfined aquifers (i.e., those connected to surface water bodies) may drop because of reduced recharge and increased rates of pumping. Municipal supply and most large-scale irrigation wells in developed countries like the US tend to be drilled into larger aquifers and at depths greater than wells supplying individual domestic users. As a result, they are less vulnerable to these problems. However, in developing nations where individual farmers or villagers rely on more shallow and easier to dig wells, and where control over their management is often less clear and well regulated, the potential danger of depletion is severe. In addition to smaller yields of water, drops in water table depths during a drought may dry up inter-connected springs and streams, especially if demand increases due to lower rainfall and higher rates of evapotranspiration. Once groundwater overdraft occurs, what is likely to follow are: reduced vegetation, more land subsidence, more seawater intrusion, and more conflicts between users who accuse one another of abetting higher depletion rates through over-pumping.

Three closely studied areas in the US – Texas, New York, and Massachusetts – reveal the range of impacts that can be expected in developed countries, and may help us calibrate how much worse impacts would be elsewhere. The Edwards Aquifer in south-central Texas, which supplies over two million people in the San Antonio metropolitan area, is already subject to highly variable rates of groundwater recharge and has undergone a steady increase in pumping rates over the last century. Concerns over climate change have prompted plans for water imports and even desalination.

Meanwhile, Rockland County, New York, which receives 78 percent of its local supply from small regional aquifers, has declared three separate drought emergencies since 1995. Drought has not even been a precipitating cause: the problem has been urban development and population growth overtaxing local groundwater coupled with failure of an aging water supply infrastructure. The Ipswich River Basin in northeast Massachusetts has experienced similar problems, relying on both surface- and groundwater for municipal and industrial supply. In recent years, summer demands have risen at precisely the time when the Ipswich experiences low flows, taxing available groundwater.

A final climate-related freshwater challenge is energy production, ranging from extraction of fossil fuels (mining, including coal, oil, and gas) to electric power generation.[10] In the US, water demands for cooling and steam generation in thermoelectric plants exceed those for agriculture. Emerging energy sources, such as bio-fuels, discussed in the previous section, as well as synthetic fuels and hydrogen, will add future demands. Ironically, as new and intermittent forms of renewable energy are added to the grid – in part, to reduce greenhouse gases that cause global climate change – additional stress on freshwater will be generated.

For example, many utilities are planning for the additional use of small-scale hydropower as a supplement to wind and solar energy sources. Hydropower is a flexible, low-cost generating source that can be used when these other renewable energy sources are not available (e.g., times of calm winds) in order to maintain electricity transmission reliability. Unfortunately, as more non-hydro renewables are added to the grids, calls for fluctuating hydropower operation may become more frequent, and may compete with other water demands. Moreover, if US electricity demand increases by 50 percent in the next 25 years (as predicted by the US Department of Energy) then energy-related water uses will also expand – a worrisome eventuality where freshwater is already scarce.

Some of the most direct effects of climate change on the energy sector will be felt through changes in precipitation and stream flow that will affect power availability and transmission system reliability. Increases in storm intensity could threaten further disruptions of the type experienced in 2005 with Hurricane Katrina, for example. Also, average temperature increases will likely increase energy needs for cooling and reduce those for warming while the reductions in groundwater levels may increase demands for energy in order to sustain pumping (another example of how water and energy demands are connected).

Connections between energy demands and freshwater are made more complex by virtue of the fact that in many countries they are made in large basins where freshwater is harnessed for many uses, including flood control, navigation, irrigation, public supply, fisheries, as well as energy production. The Tennessee Valley Authority (TVA) is a good example. Since 1934, TVA has operated an integrated system that now features nuclear, coal, and hydropower plants (figure 2.1). Its river operations include upstream storage reservoirs and locks and dams. Cold water is a valuable resource that is stored in headwater reservoirs and routed through the river system to maximize cooling efficiencies of the downstream thermoelectric plants. Reservoir releases are continuously adjusted through a highly managed system designed to produce low-cost power while providing adequate water supply and quality.   In developing nations, TVA's framework of multi-purpose freshwater management has become a model for river basin development. Unfortunately, juggling these various choices is an even more daunting challenge due to grinding poverty, aspirations to achieve rapid economic growth, and an environmental NGO sector that is often weak and poorly organized.

Sustainability and Public Engagement

Our Common Future may be one of the best known overviews of sustainability but it is not the first. Throughout history, people have sought to codify formal rules to manage water in order to allocate it fairly, amicably, and with regard to the needs of both nature and society. Not only was managing freshwater a preoccupation of ancient civilizations, but so was concern regarding the balance that should be accorded economic, environmental, and ethical considerations.

Whether the Ancient Hebrews had a term for sustainability we may never know. However, the author of the Old Testament's Book of Ezekiel certainly understood the concept as applied to freshwater when s/he wrote: "Swarms of living creatures will live wherever the river flows. There will be large numbers of fish, because the river flows there . . . Fruit trees of all kinds will grow on both banks. Their leaves will not wither, nor will their fruit fail because the water flows to them." The

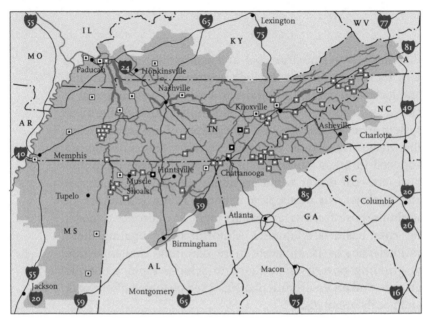

KEY: ■ = dams/reservoirs
      ▣ = Coal-fired power plants
      ▣ = nuclear plants

Source: http://www.tva.com/sites/sites_ie.htm

Figure 2.1 Tennessee Valley Authority: region of operation and power plants

late first-century (AD) figure Sextus Julius Frontinus, supervisor of the city of Rome's water supply, and manager of an aqueduct system serving over a million people, also understood the concept, as suggested in his lament: "It is plain . . . how much more our forefathers cared for the general good rather than private luxury, inasmuch as even the water which private parties used was made to serve the public interest."[11] The object of Frontinus' scorn was the wealthy and influential aristocracy whose highly-placed friends in Emperor Trajan's court could bend water regulations to suit their whims.

If Frontinus were alive today, he would probably comment

on how the powerful still exercise narrow goals in managing freshwater with too little care for the future. Two African cases exemplify this problem in different ways: Ethiopia's Gilgel Gibe III Dam, being built on the lower Omo River – a UNESCO World Heritage site, and Nigeria's Hadejia-Jama'are-Komadugu-Yobe Basin management plan. Gibe III, the third element in a massive five-part hydroelectric project on the Omo and its tributaries, is scheduled for completion in 2012. Developed under the supervision of the state-owned Ethiopian Electric Power Corporation (EEPCO), the project will generate some 1870 MW of power and will be one of the world's tallest concrete dams. Because less than one-third of Ethiopia's population has electricity, the government intends to export most of it to neighboring countries. However, with domestic demands projected to grow, the dam's symbolism is all the more compelling to some.

While the government oversees the resettlement of displaced migrants, the dam is being built by an Italian construction consortium and funded by several international agencies including the African Development Bank. Thus, many powerful stakeholders have a direct interest in its economic success. On the other side of the coin, several environmental NGOs, scientists, and academics from around the world, and in Ethiopia, charge that the entire project is poorly planned and unsustainable in three respects.

For one thing, critics charge that the project's adverse *environmental* impacts are irreversible. By reducing natural river flows, vital freshwater habitat all along the Omo, extending to Lake Turkana, an oasis of biodiversity in Kenya far to the south, will experience increased salinity (some 90 percent of Turkana's inflow is accounted for by the Omo). Gibe's reservoir will also be subject to high rates of evaporation, further contributing to Turkana's high salinity, and making it undrinkable and unsustaining to fisheries. And, the dam will wreak havoc upon natural flood cycles in the lower Omo, an isolated region whose 200,000 farmers, herders, and fishermen rely upon traditional flood retreat farming practices and fishing for their livelihoods.

In addition, in recent years the Omo has experienced long cycles of drought which many believe are a harbinger of long-term climate change. This could reduce Gibe III's effectiveness as an electricity-generating *development* project, resulting in reduced power sales and occasional blackouts. Furthermore, because most Ethiopians rely on charcoal and wood to heat their homes and cook their food, and because it would take decades for them to be connected to the dam's power grid, they will continue to deforest and denude the countryside in search of energy. While the government is seeking to reverse deforestation by reducing both charcoal and wood use, it has not devoted sufficient resources to re-allocating energy services, providing modern cooking stoves, or conducting re-forestation and other watershed restoration projects.

And finally, only a tiny fraction of the population directly affected by the filling reservoirs – comprising some eight traditional cultures including the Mursi, Bodi, Kara, and Nyangatom – has been consulted about the dam and the economic and environmental changes it will bring about. Many remain unaware of the project, and have little power to oppose it or even to modify it. In short, the project is tightly controlled by foreign corporations, investment institutions, and Ethiopia's authoritarian rulers, and few environmental NGOs or academics who oppose the project dare speak out for fear of violent suppression. The evidence clearly suggests that those who control the project are adamantly opposed to broad participation in dam-related decisions or to locally managed projects as a substitute for Gilgel Gibe.[12]

Greater potential for averting irreversible harm is afforded by a project in Nigeria's Hadejia-Jama'are-Komadugu-Yobe basin, a complex effort to reverse environmental degradation and the loss of livelihoods in an 84,000 km² basin in northeast Nigeria. Between 1970 and 1992, two projects were built by Nigeria's federal government to provide irrigation and flood control: the Tiga and Challawa Gorge Dams. From the very start, the projects suffered from a series of unexpected impacts, including slow flows in the Hadejia River and high turbidity in the Challawa.

Soon after their completion, large deposits of silt backed up behind the dams, making it necessary to release water from the reservoirs to dilute the silt. These releases led to greater downstream floods – especially during the spring rainy season – and also encouraged an infestation of typha grass, a hard to remove herbaceous plant which is notorious for clogging streams and irrigation channels. As if things couldn't get much worse, farmers and villagers living in the lowest lying parts of the basin, the wetlands, employed improvised, ad hoc measures to remove the grass, including closing some waterways and digging small channels to reduce flooding. In some cases this led to additional erosion, losses of farm and grazing lands, and severe losses of local fisheries. The number of people affected by poverty in the region increased some tenfold in the 1990s, at least partly as a result of these problems, and many irrigation systems established by the government to help farmers had to be abandoned.

In contrast to Ethiopia, where one agency is in charge of the Omo basin, decisions regarding water management in the Hadejia region are shared by several, ranging from the Nigerian federal water resources ministry to various state resource management authorities, as well as two river basin agencies – one in the Hadejia-Jama'are, and the other in the Chad. Administrative division has served as both a bane and a boon to reform. In the 1970s, separate agencies often developed their own proposals for managing parts of the basin.

And, not unlike the experience of developed countries including the US, rival agencies' plans were poorly coordinated: the same agencies charged with regulating water use are also large water users – thus, conflicts of interest were common.

In 2002, a faltering stakeholders' forum in the basin was suddenly jump-started with the support of the International Union on Conservation of Nature (IUCN), several Nigerian ministries interested in improving agriculture and water policy, and the United Kingdom's Department for International Development (DfID), which had an abiding interest in sustainable development. This forum, called the Joint Wetlands Livelihood (JWL) project, sought to institute community-level improvements in how to use water information and introduced pilot projects to demonstrate best-management practices that can restore peoples' livelihoods. A coordinating committee is brokered by high-level directors and permanent secretaries within the ministries. This committee fosters frank dialogue and exchange of ideas between local farmers and government officials. In turn, local forums made up of farmers, women's groups, and others advise the JWL and provide community-level training.

Over the past decade, the JWL has mobilized local laborers to clear typha grass blocking waterways, restored some drylands farming and fisheries in the region, and helped build *local capacity* to manage freshwater problems without resort to large, highly engineered waterworks. Federal ministries support these efforts and provide technical support to communities, while villagers applaud these small-scale ventures because they participate in their implementation. Instead of grandiose public works projects, the region now increasingly relies on "gravity flow" irrigation, small dams and irrigation works, and micro-scale investments in the current floodplain economy.[13]

If Ethiopia and Nigeria portray conventional versus novel

approaches to freshwater management, two recent Latin American cases depict a third dimension: a proactive or preventative one. The Latin American Clean Water Initiative – a collaborative effort between the UN Partnerships for Sustainable Development and Agenda 21 – seeks to provide clean, safe drinking water in a region where some 40 million people live without access to potable water and 134 million people lack adequate sanitation. Contaminated drinking water has devastating effects on especially vulnerable communities in the region; those in which most residents have incomes below the poverty line and where water-related illness is the leading cause of death.

With the help of partners from 16 countries, the Initiative has constructed water and sanitation systems including taps, outdoor washbasins, water tanks, and latrines. It has improved irrigation networks and degraded water systems. Most of all, it has involved beneficiary families in construction and repair of water systems, trained local communities in how to manage and administer these systems, equipped officials and the public with knowledge about water-borne illness issues, and instructed residents on environmental conservation and watershed restoration techniques.

While the Initiative has succeeded in building numerous sanitation and water supply projects, it remains to be seen whether the effort to build social capacity to operate, maintain, and manage these projects has really taken hold. Evidence of active community participation in the Initiative's efforts has been encouraging. In Honduras, an affiliate organization of the Initiative has provided more than 800 low-income communities with potable water and latrines, and helped form community Water Boards to train residents on the installation, maintenance, and administration of water systems, methods for protecting drinking water sources, reforesting depleted watersheds, and operating sanitation systems.[14]

A similar example of local water management focused on agriculture is taking place in the northeast Brazilian province of Ceará. In the 1990s, an interdisciplinary group within the state water management agency (COGERH) was established to institute water management reform through fostering collaboration between social and natural scientists working for a state water agency on the one hand, and local farmers on the other. The goal is to develop a series of participatory management councils in small river basins (e.g., the Lower Jaguaribe-Banabuiú River) and to negotiate water allocation agreements among users. The approach was a major departure from traditional top-down decision-making approaches to water allocation in Brazil.

Moreover, the effort to encourage so-called *técnicos* (i.e., staff scientists) to work with farmers helped the latter employ knowledge about drought and storage reservoir operations to enhance their own ability to respond to drought and flooding. This is evidenced by the growth of a more democratic approach to river basin management, a greater willingness to spread and share the risks of weather extremes and to avoid over-depletion of local supplies, and by concerted local monitoring of water conditions. Citizens are now incorporated into networks of decision making. This has helped local communities overcome the resistance of some members of the state water management authority (who now believe local farmers can manage water by themselves), and it has also placated the local water users (who are now more trusting of officials).[15]

These four cases are hardly exhaustive of all the permutations for managing freshwater. They do, however, provide a broad range of models for sustainability. The first two cases feature heavily engineered programs where sustainability was short-changed but, in one instance, environmental damage proved recoverable by adoption of democratic means of decision making. The other two cases offered inclusive decision making from the outset through local empowerment and efforts to fortify communities against threats from drought, flood, and unsanitary conditions. All four cases point to a deeper message: sustainability requires effective means of negotiation and collaboration, and the ability to share information.

Social-Ecological Approaches and Reform

If, as *Our Common Future* implies, the goal of sustainability is to ensure that natural resources are managed in ways that ensure their efficient but renewable use, and equitable distribution of their benefits, then we should seek to match up their governance with decision-making institutions of appropriate spatial scale. With regard to water, a simple way of stating this is: (1) Use watersheds as your unit of governance, (2) Convene all freshwater users together, and (3) Give them the information they need to manage. This sounds simple, but is it?

As we have seen, freshwater is subject to the whims of users, the regulations and developmental impulses of governments, and the quest for profits on the part of businesses. All institutions have shortcomings as regards the ability to promote environmental protection, social equity, or development. This is why virtually all freshwater management schemes – public or private, national or local, developed- or developing-country originated – have flaws that more often make them impediments to, rather than promoters of, sustainability. They may resist innovation due to decision-making rules that inhibit broad-based, inclusionary participation. They may defy collaboration due to habitual focus on a single mission or a limited suite of approaches to problem solving. And, they may not think that anyone who works outside of their organization, agency, or community knows anything important about water.

So, maybe the problem is less: "spatial scale of institutions" and more "good decision-making processes that fit the appropriate scale." Over the past several years, social scientists who have written about sustainability strongly contend that greater encouragement be given to developing "social-ecological systems" – ad hoc institutional arrangements that facilitate constructive dialogue and interaction among resource users and public infrastructure providers (i.e., those who build and operate engineered works like dams, irrigation systems, and power-generating facilities). Social-ecological systems may be established by law or regulation, or by markets, but they most often result from informal negotiation and collaboration among various resource users, managers, and scientists in a given region. These protagonists seek to acquire good information in order to make sound decisions (knowledge that is partly expert, partly local); embrace a comprehensive policy approach that encompasses economic, cultural, ecological, and other policy considerations; and aspire toward adaptive management.

The various experiences we've discussed in this chapter suggest that good information and sound political collaboration go hand-in-hand. Ensuring that decision makers receive and use independent, unbiased information depends on sound governance. Without collaborative partnerships and efforts to reach out to local water users, as well as efforts by top-level policy makers to build bridges between science and policy, sustainable practices are impossible to achieve. These lessons emerge strongly from Nigeria's JWL forum that encourages public education and outreach, consideration of diverse strategies for problem solving and deliberate efforts to build local management capacity. It is also shown by activities that seek to provide water and wastewater treatment infrastructure, local capacity to manage it, and the use of local knowledge and discernment to effectively sustain it (e.g., the Latin American Clean Water Initiative, Brazil's Ceará province case).

Optimal incorporation of local as well as expert information, wide-scale policy debate, and collaboration among
divergent interests rarely occur when decisions are dominated
by a single discipline (e.g., a purely "engineering" approach
to a problem), or where distinct and separate disciplines
or approaches are housed in a single set of agencies that do
not share power with others. One must not only be willing
to work with various "stakeholders" (e.g., farmers, environmental groups, community activists, minority groups, tribal
peoples) to achieve sustainability, but one must accept the
possibility that these stakeholders possess uniquely valuable
knowledge that is critical to enabling sound decisions based
on observation, experience, cultural sensitivity, and wisdom.
A national ministry may have valuable information on
climate, river flows, or ecology. However, if it cannot commu-
nicate this information to villagers in the local watershed, and
persuade them to act on it, the information will go unused,
unsustainable activities will persist, and everyone will suffer
as a consequence. The absence of participation, and information and power sharing has been a clear source of friction in
Ethiopia's Gilgel Gibe III, and an implicit barrier in managing
the unanticipated impacts of India's Tehri Dam.

The types of comprehensive policy approaches that
social-ecological partnerships envision rarely take place via
established water governance institutions. For example, in
developed societies such as the US, where innovative watershed partnerships have been formed by local officials and
environmental groups to monitor water quality, undertake
stream restoration projects through voluntary "sweat equity,"
and educate the public on watershed stewardship, the challenge of participation offers a few sobering lessons applicable
to developing countries. Foremost among these is that while
partnerships are eager to tackle serious problems at the local
level, it takes time, money, and experience to build trust and

reach agreement. Many developing countries may be at a severe disadvantage in finding the perseverance to do this, unless outside parties are willing to help (e.g., the Hadejia basin in Nigeria).

Finally, many proponents of sustainable water management advocate some form of what scientists, ecosystem managers, engineers, and regional planners term *adaptive management* – making better decisions through modifying policies in light of what we have already learned about the adverse impacts of *previous* decisions. Adaptive management encourages modest decisions, avoidance of massive structural measures such as dams where possible, the use of "real-time" environmental monitoring where feasible, and governance structures that encourage decision makers to learn from mistakes and reverse failed decisions.

As noble as this objective is, it faces two enormous hurdles. First, no society or set of water managers is rightfully in a position to "preach" adaptive management to others. Every society has made its share of unsustainable water decisions. And second, durable, publically acceptable remedies require partnerships carefully calibrated to different levels of authority, and appropriate to the specific problem at hand. Providing a just, environmentally beneficial and economically affordable local water supply system requires a different set of partnerships than would be needed for establishing a basin-wide drought protection plan.

Sustainability: Myths and Realities

In sum, the challenge of freshwater sustainability involves ensuring there is enough clean water available to satisfy the needs of the present without compromising the needs of future generations or other species. The decisions that determine if this challenge can be effectively met must be made by us – it cannot wait for future generations to answer. By the time we are certain about the impact and magnitude of changes to water supply and quality imposed by climate change, population growth, mass migrations, and poverty, it may already be too late to avert catastrophe to food supplies, energy resources, and fisheries and wildlife.

While there are many intellectual, attitudinal, and institutional barriers to overcoming this "temporal provincialism," we also need to acknowledge three myths about the control of water that further impede sustainability. While we discuss these myths in chapters 3, 4, and 5, we briefly acknowledge them here. The first myth has to do with who controls freshwater. Many argue that freshwater decisions are controlled by elites – small groups of decision makers whose influence comes from some special source of authority: for example, *knowledge and expertise* (knowing where water can be found, and how much is available for use); *monetary power* (being able to control the disposition and/or allocation of water through directing markets or buying access); or *political legal power* (using law, regulation, administrative rules, and treaties to acquire influence over the decision-making processes that govern its allocation, quality, and use).

In reality, all forms of power over water are reciprocal: they must be accepted as legitimate by others based on widely shared norms, rules, laws, market arrangements, and – most of all – mutual benefits. As we have seen, when power is *not* widely seen as authoritative, heated debate over the equity and fairness of how freshwater is managed will arise, generating conflict and defiant challenges regarding how it is controlled.

A second myth is that trans-national water conflicts are virtually impossible to resolve or amicably manage. The conventional view regarding trans-national disputes is that efforts to protect freshwater sources and to fairly allocate supplies among two or more countries generally fail in the face of unequal political power. As we saw in chapter I in our discussion of the Nile Basin Initiative, international water disputes generally entail some measure of cooperation for the simple reason that no single country can completely control the freshwater it shares with neighbors – especially if that shared resource is a river or aquifer. This does not mean that dispute resolution is easy. Again turning to the Nile – basin countries have yet to agree on an allocation formula or a mechanism for its enforcement.

Finally, public participation alone does not necessarily lead to sustainable outcomes. Participation, it must be admitted, appeals to the widely held belief prominent in democratic societies that shared control over freshwater by divergent groups, different political jurisdictions, and multiple agencies ensures policies that are fair because the interests and needs of many have to be balanced and negotiated. Unfortunately, as we will see, while participation may lead to a balance of power, it may also invite decisional gridlock. Unless there is both a means to hold various interests accountable for making and enforcing decisions, and the will to decisively address problems that require sacrifice, clear direction, and behavior change, then all the participation one can muster will not make for better or more sustainable freshwater policies.

CHAPTER THREE

Threats to Freshwater

When we harness rivers, lakes, and aquifers to quench a city's thirst, irrigate a farm, or prevent floods, we set in motion unpredictable changes. Streams may not carry as much water as they used to; the water they convey may be more polluted than in the past; and wells may dry up more quickly during drought. The good news is that many of these changes can be reversed. The bad news is that reversing them is difficult and expensive and, like the original threats, they generate geopolitical struggles over who controls water. *Watershed restoration* is devoted to repairing rivers and streams altered by these changes. It has met with varying degrees of success worldwide, as we will see.[1]

This chapter explores how efforts to attain geopolitical control of freshwater generate ongoing and persistent threats to its sustainability. When nations and individuals first cause harm, and later attempt to repair it, they engage in a struggle over whose voice will prevail in freshwater management. Genuine, fervent promotion of sustainability requires sharing power with other protagonists, and accommodating the voices of those potentially affected by threats to sustainability. We first examine cases that illustrate how we inflict harm by excluding some voices at the expense of others, and why reversing harm is difficult. We next consider a broad range of activities that inflict harm: land use, diversion, and flood abatement. Lastly, we consider some myths regarding sharing power in order to avert and repair threats to freshwater.

A Tale of Three Rivers

The Los Angeles River, a 51-mile-long stream formed at the confluence of Bull and Callabasas Creeks in the city's San Fernando Valley, was once a rustic, meandering stream in a bucolic setting. It served as habitat for species as varied as cottonwood trees and cougars. From 1781, when Los Angeles was founded, until 1913, the river also served as an urban oasis: a picturesque source of the city's water until a controversial aqueduct to the eastern Sierras was completed. Water was drawn by hand-dug *zanjas*: artfully-built ditches that carried water to homes, farms, and orchards adjacent to the plaza, the early pueblo's center of civic life.

While bucolic, it could also be capricious. Sudden downpours often caused the river to wash over its banks, ravaging homes, vehicles, bridges, and roads – and causing terrible loss of life. In the 1930s, as the city became a major metropolis, powerful civic groups who sought to promote real estate development – "boosters" in the language of the time, who were tired of managing floods – sought help from local elected officials and Congress to control the river's erratic behavior. The result was that the Army Corps of Engineers confined parts of the river to a concrete-lined channel that conveyed water to the ocean so efficiently that it remained dry most of the year. While an efficient water carrier, the Los Angeles River became a local eyesore and a symbol of declining civic pride in the city's colorful past.

After suffering for many years as a canvass for graffiti-taggers, and a backdrop for TV car chases and sci-fi movies, the straight-jacketed stream is finally undergoing an effort toward restoration that may return it to something resembling a real river again. The city, its water and power department, the federal government, and several spirited community and environmental groups, including one called "Friends of the

Los Angeles River," have formulated plans to remove 32 miles of concrete banks, re-plant native vegetation, and develop greenways and riverfront parks complete with historic markers to celebrate the river's cultural heritage, as well as flyways for sea-birds.

While it is widely acknowledged that these efforts will take decades and millions of dollars to complete, revitalization efforts face more serious geopolitical challenges. Powerful community development advocates favor gentrifying stretches of the river-front, encouraging high-end, expensive condos to be built at the exclusion of more affordable housing and the working class families that depend on it. Sharp debate over the proper balance between recreational access and job-creating tourist amenities has also arisen – pitting working-class families whose kids have few safe places to play against entrepreneurs. And some of the agencies responsible for restoring the river (e.g., the Army Corps of Engineers) are not sure it warrants the same level of environmental protection as, say, a so-called "navigable" stream that contains lots of water year-round.[2] As a powerful public works agency, connected to community leaders, the Corps has found itself at odds with vocal, determined environmental activists. Others around the world are also curious to see how well Los Angeles succeeds. Restoration of the Cheonggyecheon, a stream bisecting Seoul, South Korea, for instance, has used Los Angeles as its model for how to resurrect a river as an urban amenity.

Efforts to restore the Los Angeles River are less contentious than those facing the Rhine, another venerable stream suffering costly but reversible harm. A multinational river, the Rhine flows nearly 800 miles from Switzerland to the North Sea: passing through Liechtenstein, Austria, Germany, France, and the Netherlands, while its major tributaries traverse Belgium and Luxembourg. In the nineteenth century, the Rhine contained one of Europe's most productive salmon fisheries with annual catches of 150,000 fish. By 1958 salmon had disappeared entirely, 90 percent of the river's floodplain had been cut off by development, and severe pollution had killed off river otter in the Netherlands, seals in the Wadden Sea, and cormorant chicks in the Rhine delta. Channelization has transformed it into an artificial navigation conduit. For decades, its quality has deteriorated through potash mining in Alsace (contributing one-third of the river's salt load), runoff from quaint, neatly-tended Dutch and German dairy farms, and industrial discharges in Switzerland. Some 20 percent of the world's chemical plants line the Rhine's banks.

As environmental decline became starkly apparent, efforts to repair damaged fisheries and restore water quality were undertaken – at first in Germany, and later, throughout the basin. In 1904, an entity called the "Ruhr Agencies" was formed and charged with encouraging hydropower development to foster additional industrialization in the region and to reduce pollution and protect water supply. Finding that this combination of responsibilities was too taxing for one entity, more serious reforms were demanded. In 1950, the first real effort to restore water quality was undertaken: the International Commission for the Protection of the Rhine against Pollution, or ICPR, was formed by the Netherlands, Germany, France, Luxembourg, and Switzerland. Initially, ICPR's strategy consisted in urging common pollution standards by member states, adopting similar approaches to wastewater treatment, explicit limits on hazardous discharges, and joint research on the origins and effects of pollution. Later, ICPR advised the European Union and national governments on pollution prevention measures and sought – through formal treaty – prohibitions on discharges of especially hazardous chemicals. For its first 40 years, critics charged ICPR with being overly dependent on voluntary cooperation by member countries.

The Rhine Commission, a stepping stone for a European

Union framework to manage water quality and supply, has made good progress on trans-national cooperation. General water quality goals have been established, a common water pollution monitoring protocol has been put into place, and a negotiated oversight framework applicable to all of Europe has been set in motion (as we will see, the Danube basin has adopted a comparable framework). Nevertheless, this agreement has not gone far enough.

In the 1990s, following a spate of high-profile chemical spills, ICPR turned to a bolder river recovery strategy. Member states adopted a Convention on the Protection of the Rhine (1999) committing them to firm water quality objectives, methods for safely dispersing sediment, and restoration of North Sea fisheries. In addition, at the behest of environmental groups who charged that previous standards were too weak and industrial groups that complained about having to comply with water quality standards that varied from country to country, a participatory innovation was introduced. Environmental and business groups were invited to have a formal voice in ICPR assemblies, working groups, and ministerial councils alongside governmental representatives.

Despite these promising efforts, water quality in the Rhine remains poor, salmon have not reappeared in significant numbers, and the inclusion of civil society groups in deliberations has not altered the primacy accorded *national* management practices. In-stream flows are still managed by a variety of agencies with conflicting missions (e.g., navigation, hydropower) and cleanup efforts continue to be hampered by the reluctance of national regulators to grant ICPR independent enforcement and investigative clout. While visitors to the Rhine are initially drawn to vistas of a verdant valley filled with vineyards and castles, throughout much of its length the river remains a phosphate, nitrate, and heavy metal-laden sewer: its ecology severely tested.[3]

If efforts to restore the Rhine aim to reverse centuries of abuse, threats to China's Yangtze River pose another type of challenge: how to reverse environmental damage caused by a recently-built dam promoted by Communist Party leaders as an engine for development. Three Gorges Dam – the world's largest impoundment and the planet's biggest electricity producer – is a poignant symbol of national engineering pride. Built primarily to prevent severe flooding of the Yangtze – a stream which over many centuries has periodically overflowed its banks, causing untold damage, misery, and loss of life – the dam has also stimulated navigation and power production. Since its completion in 2005, 1.5 million hectares of land and over 15 million people have been protected from severe floods: but not flawlessly. In July 2010 the reservoir level had to be lowered to provide additional storage for torrential rains far upstream. The Yangtze now also serves as a year-round navigation channel from South-central China to Shanghai. Cargo to the East China Sea has increased from 9.5 million tons per year in 2003 to over 60 million in 2008. And, its generators produce some 22,500 MW, equal to 15 power stations without producing greenhouse gases or radioactive waste.

Impressive as these figures are, the dam's environmental and social impacts are also noteworthy, but for different reasons. Native species such as the Chinese River Dolphin and Chinese Paddlefish lost habitat and experienced dramatic population declines. Nearly 95 percent of the winter hibernating wetlands of the endangered Siberian Crane have been destroyed. And between 1.3 and 2 million people living in 13 cities, 140 towns, 1,350 villages, and over 600 kilometers of inundated river valley, have been moved into jerry-built, substandard housing. Moreover, many archeological sites have been permanently lost – their artifacts unrecoverable and their historic significance drowned beneath billions of gallons of water. Additionally, hundreds of factories, mines, and waste dumps were also flooded, generating polluted effluent and trash.

Environmental surprises also arose with the dam's completion: erosion of the reservoir's banks as well as downstream shorelines when the dam is generating large amounts of power has caused frequent landslides. Pollution, siltation and lower than normal nutrient flows have reduced annual fishery catches in the East China Sea – by upwards of one million tons per year according to some estimates. Silt build-up is especially troublesome: over time, it will reduce nutrient-laden soils in the Yangtze delta that would otherwise nourish aquatic life as well as farms, and it will decrease the amount of electricity Three Gorges Dam can generate.

Three Gorges has also been plagued by corruption, spiraling costs, and accusations that community resettlement funds were misspent – the latter leading to public protests, jailed dissidents (and a few officials), and official investigations of malfeasance.[4] After the dam was completed, the Chinese Academies of Social Sciences and Engineering, convinced that Three Gorges' environmental and societal impacts were severe and poorly anticipated, admonished the government to engage in broader discussions about the complex trade-offs involved in future large-scale energy projects. In the case of big dams, these include the risk of destroying habitat for threatened fish species, unfortunate to be sure, versus burning more coal – which causes air pollution and climate change, and may also threaten aquatic species with extinction.

Most of all – as now acknowledged because of the Science Academies' severe criticisms – virtually all vital decisions regarding site-selection, construction, relocation of local residents, environmental assessment, and daily operation of Three Gorges were made by engineers and managers who neither invited nor embraced discussion of these impacts. Had the government listened to the voices of those forced to relocate from its flood-pool, as well as others who witnessed the ecological harm caused by the dam, some of these adverse impacts might have been averted. While it is unlikely the Communist Party will repeat these mistakes anytime soon, what remains to be seen is whether current problems can be repaired, and if the government will share with non-governmental groups the opportunity to help fix them.

These cases embody three important lessons. First, when nations, regions, or cities initially develop their economies, they often place less value on the aesthetic and ecological value of free-flowing rivers than upon their control. Only later, after they modernize, do they view such freshwater resources as an amenity – not simply a commodity. Second, even after they reach this level of appreciation, the tendency to make decisions on the basis of established economic goals first, while giving far less priority to environmental, cultural, and social issues, remains largely unchanged. And third, while formerly excluded voices may now be included in efforts to fix old problems – and to prevent new threats from occurring – the same institutions that helped create the problems often remain in charge, and relinquish their power grudgingly. Urban residents may want rivers restored to a more pristine appearance. Environmental groups may seek to participate when water quality, fisheries, and local amenities are discussed. And, those dispossessed by dams may demand compensation for losses. Still, established groups and agencies will likely resist radical change. Land use illustrates this problem.

Land Use and Sprawl

Of all the activities that generate persistent threats to freshwater sustainability, land use is perhaps the most common and least appreciated. Changes in land use can have enormous effects on freshwater. However, because these impacts vary from place to place, they are often difficult to document. For example, we know that urbanization generally leads to changes in the volume of water carried by streams, their structure and shape, and even the kinds of life they can support. The experience of the Los Angeles and Rhine rivers illustrates these problems. As the former grew in population and became more built-up, residents' efforts to channel the river to abate floods changed its shape and, thus, its capacity to support fish and wildlife. In the latter case, heavy industry and farms located along its banks produced prodigious amounts of silt-laden pollutants, choking fish and killing off wildlife far downstream.

Because land use changes are place-specific, it is also hard to generalize about who is directly responsible for the freshwater harm they cause, and even harder to repair it. Urban "sprawl" – a pattern of land use characterized by low-density development such as large, paved-over shopping plazas, commercial and industrial parks, and housing subdivisions transected by roadways and parking lots – illustrates this problem. In the large and growing megacities of developing countries discussed in chapter 1, for example, two activities associated with their growth: paving of land surfaces and disturbance of soils and bedrock through construction impede the flow of vital nutrients needed by fish, accelerate storm runoff (due to greater impervious land surface), worsen stream-bank erosion, and increase flooding. Similarly, in urban areas reliant on groundwater, artesian zones tend to encourage dense settlement close to where water rises to the surface, causing groundwater contamination.

Worst of all, urban sprawl-worsened storm-water runoff caused by road building, construction, and industrial pollution nourishes algae blooms in lakes and rivers, killing fish by driving out available oxygen. Runoff also causes outbreaks of *Pfiesteria* – a microscopic fish-killing organism. And, it can cause massive nitrogen and phosphorous-infused "dead zones," technically referred to as "hypoxia," which severely curtail commercial fisheries. Such dead zones are now found along the Pacific coast of Oregon, the Gulf Coast of Louisiana, the Baltic Sea between Russia and Finland, the rich lobster fishery in the Kattegat – a patch of the North Sea between Denmark and Sweden, and elsewhere.

Worldwide, local zoning ordinances designed to regulate the location and density of various kinds of development are commonly used to protect water quality by averting runoff. Later, we will see an example of this when we discuss Chesapeake Bay. In general, these tools – by themselves – are ineffective for two reasons. First, they commonly run into opposition from property owners who insist on reserving the right to farm the way they want, apply whatever chemicals are needed to increase yields, and/or pave over their land for real estate development. Second, in developing countries especially, local governments responsible for land use regulation have little enforcement power to institute effective zoning regulations, or the resources to establish water treatment infrastructure, sanitation systems, or floodplain management plans.[5] Given the foregoing, what more can be done?

Innovative remedies to better manage the water quality impacts caused by land uses are being introduced. These remedies seek to: prevent point- and non-point-source pollution to safeguard drinking water supplies; lower water treatment costs by averting uncontrolled, poorly managed development; educate the public on the role they can play in averting land use generated freshwater harms; and most of all, employ public-private partnerships to include diverse and important voices and share responsibility for policy.

One attempt to implement locally applied measures on a national scale is the United Kingdom's *Water Conservation*

Management Strategy. Introduced in 2008, it comprises a series of measures that impose minimum water efficiency standards for new construction, promote water conservation by industry, reduce non-point pollution by agriculture, and lessen runoff that causes urban flooding through gradually replacing asphalt with porous materials for "car parks" and other properties. Activities to aid drainage and store rainwater are also encouraged by the strategy. Most significantly, the strategy depends on national government partnership with industry, homeowners, commercial property owners, farmers, and municipal authorities.

Broadly inclusive participation by stakeholders helps minimize conflict while maximizing compliance with the strategy's objectives. Meetings among local partners responsible for implementing the strategy at local levels emphasize public education and outreach, and voluntary adoption of solutions is encouraged. Interconnections between water quality and supply are touted by regional planners and emphasized in public outreach efforts. The strategy also relies on innovative economic incentives, including an enhanced capital allowance that provides tax relief for businesses and others who invest in water-saving approaches.

In the UK, as in many countries, the national government's capacity to manage private land uses that affect water quality are limited by property rights, the diversity of uses, and the varied jurisdictional responsibilities for land use regulation. Thus, the *Water Conservation Management Strategy* acknowledges that government lacks authority to institute repairs by itself. As its preamble states: "Our vision cannot be achieved by Government alone. We all need to take responsibility for ensuring that we achieve our objectives and work collaboratively to protect and enhance our water resources and manage them in more sustainable ways."[6]

An equally ambitious if less successful innovation is the

Danube River Protection Convention, or ICPDR, established in 1998 among 13 countries to improve water quality, control pollution, avert industrial accidents, restore fisheries, protect the Black Sea from land-based pollution, and achieve sustainable management of the Danube basin. The reason it has been less than successful is because it relies on voluntary "harmonization" of land use regulations and pollution prevention policies by individual countries – many of which face unique challenges in reducing land-based pollution sources. The ICPDR has also suffered from political obstacles that pit country interests against one another – complicating achievement of its goal of inclusiveness.

As in Europe's other great river, the Rhine, the Danube's aquatic life has endured centuries of abuse. Habitat loss, pollution, over-harvesting, and introduction of invasive species (the Danube is a navigable stream and an international trade artery) have endangered native fish species such as Danube salmon and sturgeon. Among the unique challenges alluded to above is decades of neglect by authoritarian governments that were stingy in providing adequate water treatment or best-management practices that would reduce runoff. The former problem has resulted in the return of wastewater generated by the more than 80 million basin residents to the Danube, mostly untreated. With assistance from the UN Development Program and the so-called Global Environment Fund, a joint effort of the World Bank and UN Environment Program, the ICPDR first focused on generating baseline data on water quality and quantity – and has used this data to generate point-source pollution reduction strategies and smarter land use runoff reduction measures. In conjunction with this approach, ICPDR has also sought to identify major sources of pollution: so called "hot spots" centered on municipalities, manufacturing centers, and agriculture.

Over 50 such areas have been identified, with industrial

pollution, toxic material dumping, and excessive nutrients (nitrogen and phosphorous) from farms and animal-feeding operations discerned as culprits. Nutrients have found their way into the Black Sea – some 500,000 tons of nitrates and 50 tons of phosphates annually. Most of the 400 mitigation projects adopted to deal with these so-called "hot spots" are designed to reduce problems which have the greatest transboundary impact through improving wastewater treatment, providing more farm conservation easements, prudently applying fertilizers, and wetland restoration and "rehabilitation," a key land use strategy to capture nutrients and serve as habitat for threatened aquatic species.

Progress has occurred. In the Black Sea, a large hypoxia-induced "dead zone" has dramatically shrunk in size and improved in quality since the late 1980s. Much of this recovery is due to closure of large animal-feeding operations and reduced fertilizer use, both resulting from the collapse of centralized economic planning. Nonetheless, conflicting country interests remain an impediment to solving water quality problems. For example, in 1977 Hungary and the former Czechoslovakia signed a treaty to build a dam and water diversion project. When Hungary halted construction due to public opposition to the project's possible environmental harm, Czechoslovakia diverted the Danube into canals for its own use. After Slovakia became independent, negotiations with Hungary resumed with the European Union serving as mediator. The International Court of Justice, asked by Hungary to intervene, ruled that Hungary was wrong to halt the dam project. The dispute continues with little end in sight. In short, the ICPDR has enhanced the voices of environmentalists and scientists in managing the basin's problems. It has not, however, entirely succeeded in overcoming traditional national interest rivalries that inhibit sustainable freshwater management.[7]

Vanishing Freshwater and Diversion

If land use is a persistent but little appreciated threat to water quality, inter-basin diversion – moving vast amounts of freshwater from one river basin to another – is a far more visible threat. It also generates far greater geopolitical conflict, often over vast amounts of territory. As discussed in chapter 1, the earliest large-scale diversions occurred in the Near East about 4,000 years ago when the Sumerians discovered how to divert the Euphrates River (in what is now Iraq) to irrigate crops and reduce reliance on the vagaries of seasonal rainfall. The major reason to undertake diversion, then as now, is to provide additional supplies to foster agriculture and provide public supply to a region with inadequate freshwater. A related motive is to promote regional economic development. This was a major inspiration for the construction of privately funded irrigation diversion in the Imperial Valley of California in the nineteenth century, for example.

While diversion entails an exchange between "catchments" (i.e., watersheds), it also moves water between *jurisdictions* – making it politically as well as ecologically problematic. Physically, diversion can be achieved through pipelines, tunnels, aqueducts, pumping facilities, or even seaborne delivery systems – an idea recently contemplated under proposals to transfer water from the Great Lakes to the Middle East in converted oil tankers, for instance, or by towing freshwater in giant seaborne bags from Turkey to northern Cyprus – an effort that has actually been attempted. One Norwegian company has even figured a way to earn a profit doing this.[8]

For the exporting region (the "diverter"), the benefits of diversion include economic compensation and better relations with neighbors. Diverters also face adverse, unintended consequences, however, especially if the importing region (the "divertee") fails to consult with the former. History is replete with such examples, most of which have had as their genesis various harms, including depletion of local water supplies, degraded fisheries, and change in the livelihoods of residents living in the exporting basin. Not surprisingly, whether potential harms caused by diversion can be averted – or corrected – depends to a great extent on how well the voices of potentially affected populations are included in decisions. Russian and Australian experiences illustrate this.

Freshwater diversion inflicts a wide range of environmental harms, from altering in-stream flow (i.e., the volume, flow, and quality of water naturally found in rivers and streams) to species transfer (the consignment of exotic fish or other aquatic species from one basin to another). Most diversions end up returning some water to the streams from which they originate. In general, if this return flow is relatively prompt and abundant, harm to fish and wildlife from low flows is likely to be less severe than if return flow is small in volume, or occurs after lengthy delay.

In the mid-1950s, the Soviet Union conceived plans for diverting northward-flowing Siberian Rivers to the arid southern part of the country. These plans included no strategy for providing return flow. That is because the objective was to irrigate the Kyzylkum desert in Central Asia with as much water as could be shipped south. Premier Nikita Khrushchev, typifying the environmental arrogance of Soviet leaders of that era, and an avid supporter, stated that his country "could not wait for nature to provide its fruits to society and that his society was ready to take those fruits . . . using its national technological prowess." Fortunately, even in a one-party dictatorship during the heart of the Cold War, geographers, soil scientists, and environmental writers, whose expertise the regime needed, hotly debated the merits of the project. Some of these critics suggested that diverting large amounts of freshwater from flowing naturally into the Arctic Ocean could lead to the melting of Arctic Sea ice and a change in global climate – this, in the 1950s! Their outspoken opposition was sufficient to delay the project for 30 years, although subsequent leaders continued to support the proposal.

In 1986, Premier Mikhail Gorbachev, the last leader of the Soviet Union, introduced the policy of "glasnost" or openness – ensuring that discussions on environmental and related issues would take place in larger public forums. This policy also had the result of legally sanctioning input from diverse citizen networks, and permitting official acknowledgement of previous mistakes and failures in the domain of environmental policy. By the late 1990s, with support from environmentalists, Gorbachev cancelled plans to divert Siberian Rivers southward.

Matters did not end there, however. Gorbachev's decision upset leaders of the newly empowered Soviet Central Asian Republics, particularly Uzbekistan and Kazakhstan, who were already faced with repairing the adverse effects of previous diversions by trying to repair damaged, drained lakes and streams. The best example of this is the Aral Sea, an inland lake that is rapidly drying up and shrinking as a result of diversion of the rivers that feed it. This practice began in 1960 in order to grow irrigated cotton and rice, and was spawned by the same environmental hubris during Khrushchev's reign which gave rise to plans for Siberian river diversion.

Central Asian leaders not only expected Siberian water imports to eventually restore the Aral Sea, but they further believed that such diversion constituted a form of compensation for the sacrifice they bore to grow cotton to feed textile mills in the Russian portion of the former Soviet Union. Furthermore, they believed, this "debt" was owed them by the Russian government as the successor state to the former Soviet Union. In 1995, after the Soviet Union's break-up, at a regional heads-of-state meeting on the Aral Sea crisis organized by the UN Development Program in Tashkent, Uzbekistan, the Russian Minister for the Environment told the presidents of the Central Asian Republics that Russia would provide them with water, either from the Volga – or other Russian rivers in Siberia. This was interpreted as re-commitment to the grandiose 1950s scheme to move large amounts of water to solve Central Asia's water problems. What Russia actually intended, however, was to sell them water from a scaled-back diversion project – if funding could be secured from the World Bank. As it turned out, the Bank rejected the proposal on environmental grounds.

In 1998, Moscow mayor Yuri Luzhkov, an aspiring national figure, revived the idea of diversion by recommending routing the Ob to Kazakhstan and Uzbekistan as a profitable venture that could also ensure stable cotton supplies. Almost imme-diately – and to a fervent degree not seen in earlier times – the Russian Academy of Sciences, led by scientist Vladimir Anykaev, condemned the proposal, charging that it would adversely affect the ecology of Uzbekistan and Kazakhstan and severely disrupt Arctic Sea temperatures – again threatening to play havoc with global climate. One lesson of this diversion scheme, which refuses to go away, is that the Soviet system's environmental hubris, a product of its authoritarian past, has not disappeared. Fixing one engineered freshwater problem by causing another is a monstrous idea that is difficult to slay.[9]

The Murray-Darling basin covers 14 percent of Australia's land area and is the country's most important agricultural region, containing over 40 percent of its farms and produc-ing some $10 billion worth of crops and livestock annually. Nearly 2 million people live within the basin and receive their water from the Murray-Darling system, while another 1.25 million living outside the basin depend on it for their public water supply. The Murray-Darling Basin Agreement (MDBA), established in 1985 by New South Wales, Victoria, South

Australia and the Commonwealth, is an effort to provide for integrated, shared management of the water and related land resources of this rich basin – the world's largest catchment system.

For decades, the single greatest problem caused by irrigation through diversion of the Murray-Darling was rising salinity levels, making farming difficult and contaminating freshwater supplies. Salinity is no minor headache: it makes freshwater taste bad, is unhealthful to consume in large amounts, retards crop growth (when it doesn't kill crops altogether), and corrodes plumbing. It is also difficult to control because most "salts" come from minerals dissolved when water is applied to soils. The salinity problem also ignores political boundaries, which is why MDBA adopted a comprehensive watershed restoration approach to repair other water quality and water supply problems facing the basin. This is the kind of restoration approach discussed at the beginning of this chapter. MDBA is empowered to coordinate state efforts to: manage drought, compensate for climate variability, control agricultural runoff, regulate in-stream flow, and avert flooding, all while providing "effective planning and management for the equitable, efficient and sustainable use of the water, land and environmental resources [of the basin]." Thus, efforts to reduce salinity are linked to other strategies to prevent waterlogging of floodplains and build-up of salts in the Murray and Murrumbidgee Valleys. The Authority can allocate water not only to control pollution and benefit water users, but it has had the power – since 1995 – to cap further diversions and even to regulate consumptive uses such as agricultural irrigation.

These powers have led to measureable improvements in in-stream flow – further improving water quality and protecting threatened fish species. Moreover, changes in the operation of dams in the basin, instituted by MDBA, have permitted better fish passage and spawning, and reversed declines in native fisheries populations while also facilitating better floodplain management. MDBA's most significant innovation, however, is political, not technical. Its "sustainable management" program employs two sets of activities that embrace public participation and community involvement as ongoing components of its overall mission. First, a built-in environmental resource assessment process evaluates the social, institutional, and cultural factors that cause salinity and other water problems. This process employs frequently updated environmental monitoring to better understand economic pressures on the basin's land and water resources and to permit savvier investments in environmental improvements. Second, a community advisory effort, begun in the early 1990s, mandates that elected citizen bodies work with local, state, and federal officials to develop "integrated" plans for the basin's natural resources.

Not surprisingly, full implementation of these ambitious plans has fallen short of aspirations. Floodplain management, for example, remains a contentious issue, in part because some of the choicest agricultural lands in the basin are subject to floods. Despite this, the MDBA is nearly unparalleled in incorporating community involvement in such a large-scale watershed restoration program – one that is rooted in efforts to rectify the legacy of water diversion primarily for irrigation. The Authority has an explicit mandate to reduce salinity and to regulate demands for scarce water which worsen the problem. In contrast to, say, Russia, this effort has successfully elevated public attention to the adverse impacts of diversion; brought together divergent stakeholders in an inclusive decision-making framework; empowered scientists, environmental organizations, and local farmers to work together in the search for durable solutions; and reversed some of the adverse impacts of past activities.[10]

Floods – Abatement or Avoidance

Flooding is a *natural* hazard caused by too much rain or snow-melt concentrating a large volume of water in one place, and in a short time. According to disaster experts, however, flooding is also a *technological* hazard: its underlying causes and consequences are man-made. This is so for three reasons. First, when we pave over porous surfaces, and then expose them to petroleum drippings from motor vehicles, chemicals from lawns and gardens, and trash, we assure that runoff will be greater in volume *and* degraded in quality. Second, when we alter streams and their floodplains by dredging, channelizing, stream straightening and shoreline development, we increase the risk of property damage and loss of life. And, finally, when we construct protective measures to alleviate flooding, we encourage more building within floodplains, exposing more property to potential damage, and generating an illusion of safety.

We have learned a lot about how to alleviate and adapt to floods, including limiting development in and around flood-plains; relocating at-risk developments; adopting early warning systems to permit those in harm's way to evacuate; and, flood-proofing homes and businesses. While these efforts are well and good, it is important to bear in mind that there is a continuing need to abate flood threats through levees and other fortified measures (so-called "structural defense"), particularly in developing countries where the poor often have no choice but to live in crowded, intensively farmed floodplains. How to do this – fairly and inclusively – is a massive geopolitical challenge.

Imagine a country the size of Louisiana with over 160 million people who live on a fertile delta coursed by three major rivers – the Ganges, Brahmaputra-Jamuna, and Meghna. Imagine, further, that this country experiences chronic flooding from cyclones, tropical depressions, and other extreme weather events nearly annually. Now imagine this country's population surging by another 60 million or so by the mid-twenty-first century, while – during the same time period – climate change raises sea level to such an extent that up to 15 percent of its population may be permanently displaced and seeking shelter in neighboring countries. Millions more may become temporarily displaced by continued storm surges worsened by rising seas. This is not science fiction – it is Bangladesh, and what it is experiencing underscores how floods are both a natural and technological hazard. These events also underscore the importance of incorporating the voices of those directly affected by flooding in order to alleviate its worst impacts.

Sea level rise has already worsened the country's periodic floods. In May 2009, Cyclone Aila struck southwest Bangladesh and India, killing over 200 people and displacing some 2.3 million. While less damaging than a 2007 storm that killed over 2,000, the country's geography makes its hard to fortify against flood. The courses of the Ganges and Brahmaputra rivers are constantly shifting, making it difficult to secure river banks and protect farmland. A World Bank project, initially backed by France, Japan, and the US, would have built some 8,000 km of dikes to control the rivers, but the $10 billion proposal ran into opposition from farmers whose land it would take. Massive Dutch-style dikes to hold back the sea – and future cyclone-induced waves – are probably even more unworkable, according to the Intergovernmental Panel on Climate Change: local soils are too unstable for such "western-style" innovations.

Fortunately, there are other options. In some areas of Bangladesh, people have begun building houses on tall stilts to evade annual floodwaters. Non-governmental organizations such as the UK-based "Practical Action" have also developed simple house designs – two-foot-high concrete plinths topped with inexpensive and easily replaced jute panel walls – that help prevent some homes from being washed away during tropical storms. CARE, the US-based charity, has helped people living along the coast rediscover forgotten farming techniques such as baira cultivation, or floating gardens, an age-old agricultural system well suited to areas that are flooded for long periods.

Salt-tolerant varieties of rice have been introduced, as well as conversion of some paddies into ponds for raising shrimp and crabs. Also, family planning efforts are beginning to show progress – fertility rates have declined by nearly two-thirds since 1977.[11] Bangladesh's recent efforts to grapple with this problem illustrate how, when the voices of those most adversely impacted by flooding are included in decisions, innovations to avert harm are more likely to be appropriately – and economically – scaled to a society's level of development. In effect, good floodplain management relocates people away from avoidable hazards *and* fortifies structures when hazards cannot be avoided.

Restoring Freshwater

At the end of chapter 2, we noted three myths about the control of freshwater. Two of these: that trans-national water conflicts are impossible to resolve or amicably manage, and that broad participation leads to sustainable policies, are relevant to our discussion of geopolitical control of freshwater and its restoration. A popular view of how to restore freshwater harm *and* reduce conflict is to encourage collaboration. We now examine three cases: one where collaboration has not alleviated problems; a second where it partly has; and a third where the verdict is still out.

The Chesapeake Bay Program USA: Collaboration or Gridlock?
In the early 1980s, several US states, the District of Columbia, and US Environmental Protection Agency (EPA) joined

together to sponsor a public-private restoration partnership to reverse threats to fish and wildlife in the Chesapeake Bay estuary, a 64,000 mile^2 drainage basin of 15 million people: the Chesapeake Bay Program. The program is internationally important because Chesapeake Bay, a large, biologically diverse, and politically fragmented freshwater estuary (some 3,600 animal and plant species across parts of six states), faces problems comparable to those being confronted in other estuaries, from the Black Sea to the Baltic: diminished water quality caused by upstream farm runoff and urban development.

Restoration efforts were initiated by a broad-based, citizen-led movement. In the early 1970s, residents of Delaware, Maryland, New York, Pennsylvania, Virginia, West Virginia, and the District of Columbia, dismayed by declines in water quality and wildlife in the bay, sought the assistance of public officials. Former Maryland Senator Charles Mathias promoted a series of fact-finding efforts which eventually led to the establishment of both the Chesapeake Bay Program and a series of formal agreements – in 1983, 1987, and 2000 – that broadly committed partners to a cooperative, integrated approach to protect its shared resources.

The bay is fed by several major streams, including the Susquehanna and Chesapeake Rivers that support numerous agricultural, industrial, and urban uses vital to the economy and ecosystem of the region. Thus, viable strategies to repair the bay targeted upstream point-source pollutants and landowner participation to address non-point runoff, including public, private, military, and agricultural lands. These initiatives rely on local governments working with landowners to develop policies to alleviate pollution.

There have been a number of impediments to making this partnership work. Nutrient pollution from nitrogen and phosphates remains high, in part because of resistance by established land users, including agribusiness interests and some urban developers, to adopt practices that could alleviate runoff-laden contaminants. Moreover, land use controls that could limit development in sensitive areas or reduce pollutant sources rely almost entirely on voluntary efforts and public education methods – termed "best management practices" – as opposed to regulatory or other binding measures. Worse, both educational and incentive programs are chronically underfunded, while land use policies vary widely from state to state. In short, firm enforceable pollution standards do not exist for runoff. While the Chesapeake Bay Program has been inclusive, it has made little progress in improving water quality. As a result, the "quarter-century campaign to restore the bay has been revealed as a costly failure."[12] Not surprisingly, the program has not been widely copied elsewhere.

Brazil – Large Dams and Preventive Restoration
Itaipu Dam, built on the Parana River on the border of Brazil and Paraguay, is the second largest hydroelectric facility in the world – after China's Three Gorges Dam. Completed in 1984, it is the culmination of a 13-year construction effort and generates some 14,000 MW, accounting by itself for fully 20 percent of Brazil's, and 94 percent of Paraguay's electrical power. The dam, built by both nations, is managed by a bi-national commission which markets the project's electrical power and collaborates on attracting developers to use the power.

While Itaipu's spinoff industries (e.g., aluminum smelting attracted by cheap electricity) has encouraged foreign investment in the project's immediate vicinity – especially by Argentine, Italian, and US investors – it has also generated enormous environmental impacts. Over 700 km^2 of old growth tropical forest was destroyed, mostly on Paraguay's side of the reservoir, when the reservoir filled and trees had to be clear-cut. Some plant species, including a rare orchid unique to this region of the South American rainforest, became extinct during construction. Moreover, some sixty thousand people, mostly native, indigenous tribes, were relocated. These were not the only adverse effects of the dam's construction. After the project was completed and power sales commenced, Paraguay was unable to use all its share of the project's electricity, but it was blocked from re-selling the surplus without Brazil's permission – the operating agreement under which power was to be conjointly marketed and sold prohibited this.

Efforts to rectify Itaipu's environmental impacts are more troublesome. During construction, mostly as a result of international pressure by environmental groups, a bi-national effort was undertaken to preserve many endangered plant species, and to salvage as much old-growth rainforest as was feasible. In effect, Itaipu's builders attempted something unprecedented in a large dam: restoring the riparian environment while the project was being built. They did this by inviting scientists to study the region, work with project builders, and advise the governments of both countries.

On the positive side, it has been estimated that over 50 percent of the region's forest that could have been lost remains intact thanks to these measures. Intensive environmental monitoring has been undertaken by both governments to prevent further damage to the impounded region's flora and fauna. One of the most innovative measures whose benefits remain in question, however, is an effort to minimize the effects of reservoir flooding on the fauna of the region by catching certain species of animals and releasing them in specially established biological reserves.

The long-term success of this effort is hard to evaluate because some species may take decades to adapt to their new habitat, and Brazil's protective forest buffer on the Parana River, intended to avert further damage, may not be adequate to provide sufficient habitat for threatened species in the region. While it is clear that damage thus far averted during the dam's construction is due to consultation with scientists and environmental groups, what remains less clear is the extent to which longer-term impacts from its operation may be irreversible – a common problem for large water projects that severely alter their local environments.[13]

Reluctant Cooperation – Israel, Palestine, and De-militarizing Water

Can trans-national freshwater be amicably managed? If protagonists believe it is urgent to do so, then the answer is yes. And perhaps – just perhaps – they can also work together to avert future harm. Israel and Palestine illustrate how this can be done. They also show the formidable obstacles in doing so.

In the long-running conflict between Israel and its neighbors, freshwater has played the role of both contested resource and military objective. Water works providing supplies for agriculture and cities have occasionally been targets for destruction or conquest. Prior to the 1948 partition that created Israel, for example, Jewish settlers often seized local infrastructure from Arab villagers to ensure adequate water for their own farms and homesteads. During that war, Israeli Defense Forces opened the floodgates of the Degania and Dalhamiya dams on the Jordan River in a tactical effort to deter Iraqi troops from entering the Jordan Valley by flooding it.

Again, during the 1967 six-day war, Israel seized the Jordan's headwaters by occupying the Banias region. More recently, land use and settlement issues have been further embroiled in conflicts over freshwater. Ariel, a city-sized Jewish settlement inside the West Bank which sits atop one of the region's largest aquifers, has been the focus of Israeli-Palestinian debate regarding its strategic location as a means of abetting continued Israeli "colonization" of Palestine.

Geopolitical advantages favor Israel. After the 1967 war Israel acquired virtually exclusive control of the waters of the West Bank and Sea of Galilee, including the West Bank's mountain aquifer: collectively giving Israel about 60 percent of its freshwater, or one billion m³ per year. Israeli settlements take about 80 percent of the aquifer's flow, leaving the Palestinians with 20 percent. While Israel claims the proportion of water it uses has not changed substantially since the 1950s, Palestinians contend they are deterred from using their own freshwater by a belligerent military power that shrouds groundwater information in military secrecy. Palestinians purchase supplies from their occupiers at inflated prices, and Israel uses five times the amount of water per capita as Palestine.

In January 2001 a "joint water committee" (JWC) made up of Israeli and Palestinian officials was established to manage water infrastructure in the West Bank and Gaza. Its charter boldly proclaimed that: "the water and wastewater sphere" must be removed from the "cycle of violence" in the region. Both sides agreed to take all necessary steps to provide water supply, including repairing, maintaining and, where necessary, replacing water supply and treatment infrastructure, and mutually responding to community demands to repair water mains. They also promised to encourage the public to desist from damaging water supply infrastructure, and not to harm or interfere with personnel engaged in the repair, maintenance, or operation of water and wastewater infrastructure.

Surprisingly, the agreement works modestly well for four reasons. First, it is the culmination of a negotiating effort that began in 1995 with Israel's promise to increase water supplies to Palestinians by 28 million m³ per year. Second, the agreement is mutually verifiable and, thus, transparent: each party knows how much water is being used locally, and where it goes. They also know how much wastewater needs to be treated to protect the health of both Israeli and Palestinian settlers. Third, the agreement is pragmatic. Early on, negotiators agreed that larger questions of territorial sovereignty, while un-resolvable in the short term, should not be permitted to impede pressing water issues. Related to this is appreciation on the part of protagonists that the issues being managed are precisely those that – on the trans-national level – help minimize larger conflicts. These include providing a reliable infrastructure to distribute water equitably, empowering citizens to monitor water problems, build and maintain their own water works and treatment facilities, and anticipate threats to water quality and supply. Finally, the agreement acknowledges that the water supplies of both nations are "intertwined and inseparable." Threats to any part of the system harm Israeli and Palestinian communities. Similarly, efforts to improve and maintain an uninterrupted water supply by one side provides water security to the other.

Benefits aside, the JWC remains precarious. Meetings among the principals are rare, water lines continue to feed new Israeli settlements – despite Palestinian objection – and groundwater yields continue to decline. Moreover, criticisms of alleged Israeli manipulation of water data persist, while widespread pollution and inadequate drought management fester in the West Bank and Gaza. In 2009, several environmental organizations, including Friends of the Earth, released a communiqué condemning the Joint Water Committee for failing to provide ample supplies to the Palestinians and inadequately protecting water quality. Calling for its replacement by a model water agreement that would repose equal power and responsibility in both sides, the communiqué amplified one acknowledged limitation of the JWC – because Palestinians receive less water than do Israelis, they have less incentive not to pollute shared supplies.[14] This illuminates a central challenge of trans-national cooperation: without bona fide power-sharing based on equal voice and equitably shared benefits, conflict will likely persist, and with it, the likelihood of future harm.

Realistic Fixes

At the beginning of the chapter we stated that repairing freshwater harm is both expensive and difficult and can only be achieved through genuinely inclusive participation. Peasants in China's Yangtze basin, Palestinian villagers in the West Bank, Brazilian tribes along the Parana, and leaders of Central Asian republics that were formerly a part of the Soviet Union all share this lament.

Despite this underlying similarity, the freshwater disputes we have examined are also characterized by important differences. Chief among these is that they are either low or high intensity in character. The latter are high-stakes, intractable competitions resulting from ideological differences and refusal to share control. The Israeli-Palestinian conflict is an example. To some extent, so too are the problems faced by the Danube and Rhine basin states, though to a lesser degree. Floodplain management in Bangladesh and salinity management in the Murray-Darling basin have not been characterized by such polarized views. These "low intensity" disputes may be described as managerial conflicts over allocation, resource oversight, and logistics – i.e., Who fixes things when they break?, How much restoration can we afford?, and What's the best means for achieving it?

Another significant difference is that, even when parties agree to the need for common solutions, the absence of collaborative tools spanning watersheds, agencies, or even countries can impede agreement. Water policy experts distinguish between "first" and "second" order disputes. The former are single purpose problems managed by specialized entities.

An example would be management of Itaipu Dam by a bi-national commission. Another would be restoration of the Los Angeles River. Second order problems, by contrast, straddle watersheds and even entire countries. They are managed by multiple authorities whose rules, regulations, and perceptions differ sharply (e.g., Chesapeake Bay restoration, post-Soviet republic diversion proposals, water-sharing between Israel and Palestine).[15]

While it would be easy to suggest that second order issues are intrinsically harder to solve, it would also over-simplify the truth. In both first and second order disputes, protagonists must become convinced that the risks of inaction are greater than the costs of cooperation – this was true in the Murray-Darling basin, for example. As the Chesapeake Bay case shows, however, while water quality problems compelled parties to initially collaborate, the perceived cost of solutions has deterred decisive action. By contrast, as the UK's *Water Conservation Management Strategy* shows, a multi-jurisdictional solution to a second order problem is possible to attain if the strategy employs methods that induce parties to participate. Tax breaks, economic incentives, and water saving approaches are examples of such methods. Moreover, some first order restoration cases (e.g., Los Angeles River, Three Gorges Dam, Danube basin) may still pit divergent interests against one another in ways that lead to impasse. This is especially likely if some of these interests are historical victims of exclusionary policies that gave them little voice in water management – even if the degree of exclusion varies.

In conclusion, successful restoration efforts do three things. First, they achieve a clear consensus among parties over responsibilities for fixing problems. This consensus is accompanied by a dedicated flow of fiscal and administrative resources to solving basin restoration problems. An example of a successful case drawing on this was the Murray-Darling, in which the joint federal-state basin authority has been empowered to impose drought management policies; place controls on agricultural runoff; regulate stream flow, flood flows, and water withdrawals; and engage in comprehensive land use planning. To a more limited extent, the Israeli-Palestinian joint water authority is based on a comparable, if more tenuous consensus – and over a much smaller and more limited range of activities (i.e., public water distribution and treatment infrastructure).

By contrast, the Rhine and Danube basin initiatives – and the Chesapeake Bay restoration efforts – display little coherent authority for basin-wide management. There is no central agency with firm authority to supplant or supersede the regulatory powers of established single-jurisdictional agencies; and they are unable to compel changes in land use that could beneficially reduce runoff pollution. Likewise, unlike the successful cases cited above, the only resources available for fixing problems are those allotted voluntarily by country participants.

A second feature shared by successful restoration efforts is the ability to draw on a set of collaborative tools that span political jurisdictions that are engaged in watershed management. Again, in the Murray-Darling case, an ongoing resource assessment process which evaluates salinity "inputs" through frequent environmental monitoring, coupled with a community advisory effort consisting of elected citizen advisory groups, helps ensure collaboration and public consultation. While by no means perfect, both tools ensure integrated basin-wide planning that encompasses a wide range of concerns.

By comparison, the Israeli-Palestinian joint water agreement's conciliatory tools – consisting of local officials meeting in common discussions – are too infrequent to make much headway on underlying issues, and water data on the region's aquifers, mostly held by Israelis, is neither commonly shared nor altogether transparent. And, by further contrast, while the Rhine basin initiative incorporates non-governmental groups in established decisional forums, as we saw, collaboration is not reinforced by strong trans-national authority.

Third, effective restoration efforts tend to embrace a basic principle of adaptive management (see chapter 2) – they seek to induce parties to cooperate in restoration efforts by empha-sizing the economic and community development benefits of restoration, as well as their environmental gains. And they emphasize how basin management costs can be reduced through repair and restoration of natural riparian functions – Friends of the Los Angeles River have slowly succeeded in building public support by making a similar case. To some extent this is what the Chinese Academy of Sciences and the Danube Basin Commission seek to do in their efforts to better characterize water resources, monitor environmental condi-tions, and learn from the mistakes of previous large water and agricultural projects (e.g., Three Gorges and ICPDR restora-tion efforts).

It is notable that proponents of the Chesapeake Bay Program initially predicated their efforts on a broad-based citizen driven program that, by encouraging reductions in nutrient pollution through voluntary adoption of land use practices, would also bring down the costs of pollution abate-ment. Ironically, however, low "front-end" investments in educational and incentive-based initiatives backfired by failing to exploit the inclusiveness of the program's goals.

Putting it all together – successful restoration, in the words of a recent United Nations Environment Program (UNEP) report, "aligns governance to the global challenges of sustain-ability" by integrating activity sectors affecting water supply and quality, coordinating overall implementation of efforts by government agencies and non-governmental entities, and articulating the urgency of the need for change. This is not a pipe dream or an impossibly lofty goal – it is an eminently practical one, as we have seen in various cases in this chapter. As this UN report notes, it requires streamlining decision making – especially across national boundaries (an effort attempted with varying success in the Rhine and Danube basins and Israel-Palestine), formally institutionalizing the role of civil society groups in decisions in order to embrace the participation of under-represented groups (a lesson in Los Angeles and at Three Gorges Dam), encouraging private-public partnerships (e.g., Chesapeake Bay, Los Angeles, Itaipu), and explicitly articulating sustainability as an objective of water resources development and management (not unlike what Bangladesh has tried to do with flood alleviation). We will revisit the ethical implications of these strong, unbridled policy commitments in chapter 5. But before we do so, in chapter 4 we discuss a further complicating issue in all of this: water ownership and the growing role, worldwide, of efforts to privatize water supply.

CHAPTER FOUR

Who's in Control?

For many of us living in developed countries, freshwater is so cheap and easy to obtain that we often take for granted its availability and purity. As far as we are concerned, freshwater is supplied by taps marked "hot" and "cold." Beyond this, where it comes from, and how it is delivered and treated, is not something we worry very much about. For millions of people around the world, however, access to potable water is both difficult and costly. Moreover, many of the world's poor view provision of freshwater for their homes and places of work to be unjust and inequitable. This view extends to the price they pay, how charges are levied, and the value of what they get for their money – the safety of their water supply.

This chapter examines the different ways freshwater is sold, controlled, and delivered by public utilities, private companies, and "mixed" arrangements. We consider how various providers balance efficiency, fairness, and environmental stewardship. We first examine the implications of freshwater provision by corporate and non-corporate vendors. We consider whether private ownership reliant on capitalist models of profit and investor return is consistent with the goals of environmental protection and social justice. We then consider whether buying, selling, or leasing water rights enhance or decrease its sustainability. And we also explore how transformation of freshwater into a personal commodity – the bottled water fetish – diminishes freshwater supplies and degrades the environment. We conclude by considering the challenges facing all providers in ensuring fairness and public acceptability.

The Worth of Freshwater

As we recall from chapter 1, the cost of freshwater was a source of conflict in Cochabamba and La Paz, Bolivia over a decade ago. That country's short-lived experiment in privatization led to violent protests because water rates not only skyrocketed but they accounted for a huge proportion of people's monthly earnings. Moreover, residents were even charged for water taken from their own wells! In effect, corporate entities held exclusive control over local supplies, yet could not be held accountable for the price they charged, or their methods of control.

Bolivia is not alone in experiencing these problems. The United Nations recently found that in most developing countries, the poor spend a significantly higher percentage of their household income on water than those in industrialized nations. In fact, the poorest households expend anywhere from 3 to 11 percent of their income on water.[1] Worse still, the water they purchase is often of dubious quality because it is provided by small-scale, informal, private distributors who charge whatever the market will bear, while employing the most rudimentary of treatment methods, *if* they employ any at all.

How charges for freshwater are levied can also be contentious. Consider the situation recently faced by residents of Salta Province, Argentina, who were forced to purchase and install household meters to gauge the amount of water they consume. Utilities imposed this rule because they claimed they were running short of cash to repair and maintain local water systems. Adding insult to injury, at the same time local utilities mandated metering, they also began aggressively tracking down delinquent rate-payers, regardless of their financial predicament. They also significantly raised charges for freshwater on all rate-payers. What really irked residential users, however, was fear they would be wrongly charged for "excess" metered usage when, in fact, the culprit was poorly maintained, leaky plumbing. As a result, protests – and even vandalism – arose throughout the province, and many refused to install meters.[2]

Finally, the value of publically supplied freshwater is a serious, yet little appreciated problem, especially for many under-represented groups. A telling example is the prolific and growing use of bottled water by the poor, which we discuss later in this chapter. Many believe that tap water is impure and causes illness. And, studies in the US, for example, show that many Latinos (as well as Asian-Americans) – especially recent immigrants – resist tap water use for their children. One explanation for this is long-standing distrust of tap water purity in Latin America and East Asia. Another explanation is recent reports of dangerously contaminated public water supplies in heavily Latino communities such as Santa Ana, California, as a result of uranium, fertilizer, and raw sewage detected in small but harmful quantities.[3]

Disputes over high water prices and contentious water-levying methods, coupled with doubts over the healthfulness of tap versus bottled water, underlie a larger geopolitical problem. While decision makers around the world justifiably worry about acquiring water to support growing populations and their increasingly profligate uses, how this water is provided – the equity of its allocation and its perceived purity – are, to many citizens, more important issues. This fact underscores the importance of transparent, inclusive decision making by public and private vendors alike.

Private and Public Provision

Amidst the flurry of claims and counter-claims regarding who owns, controls, and manages the planet's freshwater

– and what difference it makes – are two little appreciated facts. First, public and privately owned providers share several geopolitical similarities. Second, the distinction between the two provision systems can easily be overstated. Regarding the first issue, public and private providers usually exercise a monopoly over water provision in their regions of operation. Economists sometimes refer to this as "economy-of-scale." The greater the area covered, and the more exclusive the rights to cover it, the cheaper it is for a water provider to build, maintain, and manage the infrastructure which serves that region. Both also operate under legal charter from government and impose charges upon users, even if some of their revenues (especially in the case of public providers) come from taxes.

Regarding the second point, in both public and privately owned systems, providers receive their supplies from state-owned reservoirs and groundwater basins, and water is delivered wholesale via dams, reservoirs, aqueducts, wells, and pumping stations built and maintained by government agencies. Moreover, the state usually administers these projects through its control of various river basin and groundwater management authorities. This is why we use the term "mixed" control, and why we caution against simplistically distinguishing public from private provision. Even in places where retail delivery of freshwater is controlled by private enterprise, the actual "production" of freshwater remains in the hands of the state.

So who – and what – are public water providers? They are special government districts that employ a combination of tax revenues, bonds, and charges levied upon users to purchase water from other public or private suppliers (e.g., government agencies that operate dams and reservoirs, or farmers, ranchers or industries willing to sell unused water). In turn, they sell retail water supply to residential, commercial, and other customers. They also build and operate the water treatment and local delivery infrastructure needed to ensure the quality and reliability of that supply.

By contrast, private providers are typically stockholder-owned, for-profit enterprises that supply and sometimes treat wastewater. They levy fees on users calculated to cover the marginal costs of providing water services (i.e., provision and treatment), and to provide an additional return-on-investment to shareholders. The latter makes them different from public water utilities. Like public water utilities, however, they control the retail provision and delivery of water supplies, and they even try to manage user demand by various means.

Worldwide, private provision of freshwater is one of the most rapidly growing business sectors. While there are many reasons for this phenomenal growth, the most important is that availability of private capital is widely seen as necessary to meet the growing demands for clean water, especially in developing nations. These demands have strained publically financed efforts to maintain, repair, or expand water supply infrastructure; compete for precious government revenues in countries facing a diminished tax base due to worldwide recession; and are viewed as a palliative for the ever-increasing costs of water treatment.[4]

The range of private provider activities is vast, and extends from the acquisition of local water rights to the purchase of local supplies by large corporations who, in turn, marshal vast amounts of labor, capital, and technology to manage freshwater provision. Not surprisingly, it is also a trans-national enterprise. Thames Water, for instance, one of the largest retail water providers in the UK, is actually a German-owned company with some 70 million customers throughout the world. Since the early 2000s, it has begun selling its developing nation assets because they are not viewed as sufficiently profitable. Meanwhile, France's "big-three" water companies (see below), among the largest private freshwater providers in the world, have an economic reach extending to former French colonies and other developing nations. *Suez Lyonnaise des Eaux* has 115 million customers in over 130 countries, while *Vivendi Environnement* serves 110 million customers in over 100 nations.

The dramatic growth of privatization has prompted questions regarding political accountability, economic fairness, and the willingness of vendors to vigilantly prioritize public health and other community concerns above handsome returns on investment. While these issues have been raised in many developing countries where privatization has become a common approach to water management, surprisingly, they have not been as vocally expressed in developed countries with longer privatization experience.

Privately owned and operated water utility companies are common in much of Europe. With roots in the early nineteenth century, private, for-profit companies operate some 80 percent of France's municipal water services and provide local distribution, wastewater treatment, and water sales and marketing. Three corporations dominate the French market: *Vivendi Environnement*, which controls 50 percent of France's waterworks, *Suez Lyonnaise des Eaux* (with a 25 percent share), and *Saur/Bouyages* (10 percent of water supplies). The remaining 15 percent of the country's water supply is municipally owned and operated.

Despite the fact that "retail" municipal water providers in France are mostly privately owned, the French government manages and controls large waterworks, including dams, reservoirs, and levees. The state also oversees the "wholesale" distribution (i.e., withdrawal and diversion) of water through an extensive system of river basin authorities – there are seven in all of France. These have supreme authority over water quality standards and their enforcement through an elaborate set of regulations and polluter charges. Moreover, local governments control local infrastructure – treatment plants and local delivery pipelines – through so-called "inter-municipality drinking water associations" which ensure that private companies operate as partners of local governments. These associations also facilitate public review of major investment and infrastructure decisions through public hearings. The "mixed" character of French water utilities is underscored by another feature: the French government owns the largest equity share of *Saur/ Bouyages* – an investment decision intended to ensure that the company remains French-owned and managed.[5]

The UK, Spain, Hungary, Portugal, and the Czech Republic also have sizeable private water suppliers which, like those of France, operate within a "mixed" management system. Germany, Italy, Poland, Portugal, and Slovakia, by contrast, have far smaller but vital private water provision sectors. In 1973, the United Kingdom Water Act established a regional system of water provision comprising ten water authorities responsible for delivery of retail water and treatment services. Since 1989, these authorities, corresponding to major basins or "catchments," were granted further authority to establish some 35 investor-owned water utilities with exclusive monopolies within their service areas. Like private companies providing electricity and gas in the UK, they are regulated cartels: they compete for investment funds in private equity markets, but their rates and services are reviewed by a national Office of Water Services.

Because they operate as capitalist enterprises designed to earn a profit in excess of their operating costs, in part to repay investors and to raise additional capital for re-investment in infrastructure, private water companies tend to be somewhat more efficient and reliable in their operations than are public providers. Reliability emanates from the fact that they are able to undertake more effective upkeep by being able to charge more than public utilities for the same services.

Table 4.1 Comparative charges for water – four countries		
Country	Cost per m³ (in US dollars)	Public or private providers predominate?
France	1.23	Private – 3 dominant companies
United Kingdom	1.18	Private – 35 vendors
United States	0.40	Public
Canada	0.51	Public

Source: Watertech Online (2001), Table 4: Comparison of water pricing in developed countries', reproduced in *Water for People, Water for Life: the United Nations World Water Development Report – Executive Summary*. 2003. Paris; UNESCO-World Water Assessment Programme, p. 27.

In France and other European countries, where private ownership of retail water provision predominates, lower per capita water consumption is one result. While there are many variables affecting the price of water, it is significant that the retail price of water in France and the UK, two countries where privatization has taken hold, is two to three times more expensive than the US and Canada – where public providers are more common (see table 4.1).

Efficiency and reliability are important, but is privatization socially just and environmentally sustainable? Four major criticisms have been lodged against private providers. First is the claim that they are less responsive to public demands for equity, safety, and cost. The International Union for the Conservation of Nature (IUCN), for example, frequently raises this charge in discussions of the challenges facing developing countries in providing water for their growing populations. IUCN and other international non-governmental organizations project a global water supply crisis and worry that privatization is transforming water into a commodity that provides material gain for profit-making enterprises, but fails to regard freshwater access as either a human need or human right. IUCN also charges that many of the international organizations which serve as global forums for discussion – and potentially for setting global standards regarding both water quality and quantity – are more preoccupied with the interests of private vendors than with the needs of citizens for access to clean water. It is important to bear in mind, however, that this criticism is made of private providers that operate in *developing*, not developed countries. We will return to this issue at the end of the chapter.

Second, critics charge that public participation in decisions regarding pricing, service, and access is sharply limited because policies are set by corporate boards advised by business managers – not by politically sensitive elected officials. The result, especially in developing nations where the capacity to regulate private enterprise is weak, and where global financial entities encourage greater private investment to reduce public indebtedness, is that public goals regarding water are held in lower regard than profit. As supposed evidence, two factors are often cited: first, in the US, where only 14 percent of municipal water supplies are privately owned, water is more expensive in those systems; and second, privatization discourages water conservation and encourages higher consumption so as to maximize profit.[6]

Third, private providers' operations are less transparent to the general public than is the case with public providers. This criticism most often arises when a public provider relinquishes control to a corporate entity. Once control over local supplies and their provision are turned over to private companies, or even when plans to do so are contemplated, enterprises may shield their operations to protect proprietary interests. When this occurs, in turn, local political support for privatization often erodes, and public officials may have a change of heart. This situation has arisen in recent years in Pune, India and Karachi, Pakistan, among other places.

Fourth, privatization is criticized on geopolitical grounds.

Critics note that, for perhaps the first time in history, the potential for transforming water into an article of trade that can be bought and sold by multinational corporations, who can then move it across vast distances, is more far-reaching than at any previous time. Globalization may also generate a financially lucrative market for investment that allows the marketing of water without nationally imposed trade restrictions: a benefit for water vendors and their stockholders (e.g., Thames Water, Vivendi), but not for local consumers.

All four criticisms hinge on generalizations that may, in specific instances, be true. Like all generalizations, however, they rest upon contestable assumptions. These include: private vendors always seek and obtain full cost recovery on investments; investments always yield a profit; and there is an inherent contradiction between private profit and public good. We will revisit these issues at the end of the chapter.

Public Provision – the Utility Model
While the US is often regarded as the archetype of the "public utility" model for water provision, this was not always the case. Until the early twentieth century, private vendors were the norm, not the exception. Private investors owned municipal water companies in many large American cities including New York, Philadelphia, and Los Angeles. The shift toward public ownership had two major sources. First, beginning in the late nineteenth century, farmers in the West banded together to form irrigation districts, a type of farm-cooperative organization, in order to secure reliable supplies. They were motivated by the fact that vagaries of climate and water – coupled with potential for conflict over scarce supplies – compelled them to cooperate to equitably share what little water they had.

Second, serious public health episodes, including outbreaks of cholera and typhoid fever in large American cities

– New Orleans, Philadelphia, and New York most notably –
and caused by contaminated water supplies, led the public to
support formation of special government districts to regional-
ize water provision. These districts were empowered to avert
dumping of raw sewage into wells and rivers and to develop,
and divert pristine water sources for urban use. These innovations were so successful that by the early twentieth century,
the public water district – for irrigation and urban supply –
became the most popular way to provide water in the US.[7]

Like private water vendors, public water providers supplement user fees with taxes and bonds to raise capital for major
construction. Typically, they also employ a three-part strategy
to plan for future needs: assessing demands, exploring alternatives to meet them, and estimating costs for each alternative.
Demand assessment involves projecting growth in economic
activities as well as population. The former is a more direct
indicator of water needs and desired quality. Some types of
manufacturing use large amounts of water, but do not necessarily require potable quality (e.g., petroleum refining). Thus, a
community that anticipates building a new refinery, but which
expects to realize little residential growth, may need additional
water (it takes approximately 77,000 gallons of water to refine
100 barrels of oil) but no new treatment capacity.

Since the 1990s, and at the behest of state governments
in the US, a number of water utilities have undertaken
efforts at water supply "regionalization," a means of com-
bining existing assets and broadening the suite of available
options. Regionalization can reduce per-unit-of-water costs
falling upon a single community or utility district; minimize
adverse environmental impacts by encouraging building of
fewer reservoirs, distribution, and treatment systems; and
spread the costs of new projects among several jurisdictions.
Regionalization can also widen the array of supply alternatives,
including, for instance, new pipelines or other connections to

existing water sources, altered or enlarged impoundments, recharging aquifers with surface flows, water harvesting (an innovation that stores storm water runoff in special off-stream ponds), and – increasingly – measures to better conserve water. Thus, it can enhance the kinds of efficiencies that private vendors achieve through higher user charges.

As regards sustainability, public water utilities face three challenges. First, the same economies-of-scale that allow public utilities to keep prices low often constrain them from pursuing supply-and-demand management innovations, because they operate on narrow earnings margins. As a result, public infrastructure often suffers from age, neglect, and lack of maintenance, especially in older urban areas. Moreover, economies-of-scale sometimes make long-term planning difficult. Amortization costs (water infrastructure is designed to last a long time) are a fixed obligation that consumes a lot of revenue. Together with the need to vigilantly monitor regulatory compliance, and to conduct detailed engineering and feasibility studies for virtually any improvement to infrastructure, they may have little initiative to foster innovation.[8]

Second, because publically owned water utilities regard freshwater as a public good, an additional challenge they face is that water prices tend to be subsidized by taxes paid by individuals and corporations that may not be direct beneficiaries of the services they provide. Moreover, because they aim to keep prices fairly low, even when they raise rates in an effort to encourage conservation, they often lack sufficient "price elasticity" to encourage dramatic reductions in use. And, being political entities with appointed or sometimes even elected boards of directors, they tend to rely on public education and outreach to encourage water savings – especially during drought.

Third, "unaccounted-for-water" losses often arise in publically owned systems. Estimated by subtracting the amount of metered water from that which originally left the treatment plant, these unaccounted losses have many causes. The most common are leaks. The American Water Works Association claims that leaking public water systems in the US commonly lose up to 20 percent of their total deliveries. Small and large utilities tend to lose the most (17 percent on average), while medium-sized utilities lose the least (12 percent). Inaccurate water metering or the absence of any metering can also cause losses. Public utilities agree on the importance of tracking, reporting, and correcting losses in service lines and plumbing fixtures in order to conserve scarce supplies, extend infrastructure life, and safeguard revenues for future repair, maintenance, and system expansion. However, since they operate on low earnings margins, and the cost of water remains inexpensive, repairs to avert losses are frequently neglected.

In urban areas in developing countries, unaccounted-for water is a far more acute problem, and includes leaks and other failures in wastewater treatment systems. Leakage rates of 50 percent are not uncommon. Moreover, urban public water systems' user charges often barely cover operation and maintenance costs, leaving practically no funds for modernization and expansion. A recent survey of such systems in 132 cities in high-, middle- and low-income countries found that 39 percent did not recover even their operation and maintenance costs (true of 100 percent of cities in South-East Asia and the Maghreb). In addition, because of inadequate or deferred maintenance, municipal water utilities are the main polluters of surface waters in many East European, Caucasus, and Central Asian countries, where up to 90 percent of nitrogen and phosphorus discharges into the Black and Caspian Seas originate from municipal wastes, as we noted in chapter 3.[9]

Public providers now frequently employ integrated resource planning (IRP) in order to better manage water demands and augment supply. IRP is pursued chiefly in communities

facing rising water supply costs, demand growth, environmental pressures, and political opposition to building new
sources of supply. In the US, it has been adopted mostly,
though not exclusively, in communities in the West where
supplies are especially precarious due to climate.

There are two major hurdles that must be overcome to
permit effective adoption of IRP. First, utilities have to integrate environmental engineering, public health, financial, and
social and economic considerations into planning. This is a
difficult challenge to overcome given the financial barriers to
innovation previously noted. Again, private, investor-owned
water providers may be in a better position to afford to conduct sophisticated needs analyses that would result in the
screening of feasible alternatives and generate scenarios for
reducing demand. Public water utility districts might not be
as capable of undertaking such analyses without regionalization. However, these public suppliers often face a fragmented
system of water governance. Rate-payers may, in principle,
support regional cooperation, flexible water supply alternatives, and innovative conservation and wastewater re-use
programs as a means of providing additional supply. In practice, however, communities often fear "regionalizing" plans
out of fear that they will lose political control over local supply.

Second, many innovative supply and demand-side options
– including wastewater recycling and desalination – face
large public acceptability hurdles. Variable rate systems that
charge more for higher rates of water use, and mandatory
water appliance retrofitting or other conservation measures,
coupled with the use of direct metering of households, may
penalize low-income households by ignoring their ability to
pay for water – even while forcing them to install high-cost,
lower-water using appliances. Conservation rate systems
under IRP – called "increasing bloc rate" systems – generate
other concerns as well, including: how individual household

budgets eligible for "conservation" rates are calculated; skepticism regarding whether increased rates are revenue neutral; whether customers are rewarded for efforts to conserve; and the high cost of enforcing conservation efforts.[10]

Water Marketing – Selling Sustainability

There is another aspect to the "ownership" of freshwater that is often overlooked – freshwater rights. In most countries water rights accrue to those who own land adjacent to, or above (in the case of groundwater), a river, stream, lake, or aquifer. These rights are important for many reasons. From the standpoint of ownership, they are especially significant because they permit marketing of water as a commodity that can be bought, sold, and, thus, transferred from one location to another.

Most water rights systems are based on property rights. In what are called riparian legal systems such as those found in much of the US, Australia, New Zealand, Canada, the UK, and even parts of Africa and India, if one owns land adjacent to a watercourse, such as a river, stream, or lake – or that overlies an aquifer – local custom, as well as many courts of law, support the right to the use of that water in a reasonable manner. This means that adjacent watercourses are to be kept clean and reasonably useable by upstream users so as to minimize harm to those living downstream. At the same time, riparian rights systems do not afford landowners an absolute right to a given *quantity* of water. For this reason, riparian systems do not easily permit the sale or lease of water rights from one landowner to another.

In the American West, the Iberian Peninsula, and much of Latin America, water rights are based on some variant of what is called the doctrine of prior appropriation – simply stated, whosoever first stakes a claim to land adjacent to freshwater has the first right to its use. This principle is better known as: "first in time, first in right." While based on property rights, in contrast to the Anglo-Saxon system of riparian rights, prior appropriation furnishes landowners the ability to buy, sell, or lease water rights in specific quantities and for explicit time periods.

In both riparian and prior appropriation systems, which accord rights to water to individuals – and in *communitarian* water rights systems such as those found among Native American tribes or traditional communities in sub-Saharan Africa and parts of the Middle East – there remains a large role for the state in water marketing. This role includes determining whether water can be diverted outside a basin; where to build storage projects for public supply, irrigation, power generation, flood control, and navigation; and what water quality standards should be imposed to protect public health and ecological resources. This role has proven to be important in decisions to employ marketing as a means of serving public ends.

While water marketing has long been employed by farmers and ranchers, in recent years, there have been growing pressures worldwide to buy and sell water in order to move it from lower to higher valued uses: those, in other words, that are considered of high public priority, such as protecting endangered or threatened species, or providing drinking water for a city. A good example of this is seen in Australia. Having less than 20 million people in an area the size of the US, but being almost uniformly arid (with the exception of some coastal areas), Australia has long faced the challenge of providing a stable water supply. Since the 1980s, New South Wales and South Australia have embarked on an extensive system of water markets which effectively buy and sell water on formal "water exchanges." These exchanges permit water to be transferred from both water-rich regions – or from less-populated areas where agricultural interests have secured control of riparian water rights previously used by farms and ranches

– to other agricultural interests or cities that have greater need for water, and who can afford to purchase it. The advantage of water marketing is that it affords a high degree of flexibility in water management.

In the US, water marketing tends to take place in Western states, where appropriation law makes possible the transfer of large volumes of water from, say, rural areas with declining agricultural activity to cities, as well as from agriculture to "in-stream protection" needs. In a number of states including Oregon, Washington, California, Montana, Texas, and Nevada, environmental organizations with long-standing traditions of purchasing or leasing land from private landowners for conservation easements and habitat protection areas, such as the Nature Conservancy, have begun buying up water rights in order to protect fish and wildlife. Aquatic ecosystems may benefit from water markets when in-stream rights are purchased in order to satisfy environmental regulations or to protect endangered species. Marketing may also encourage water efficiencies through, for example, switching to low water demand crops or more efficient water delivery methods.[11]

Water marketing requires a large infrastructure for moving water. It also requires a water rights system that allows buying and selling of water. This is more complicated than may at first appear to be the case. Appropriation law makes the buying and selling of water easier than does riparian law because, in the former, those who possess water rights are assured the use of a specified quantity of water. With a defined right to water, an appropriator can transfer that right to another at a stated price. In riparian systems, by contrast, rights to water are to its access, not usually an entitlement to a specified quantity that can be withdrawn. In Australia, the creation of marketing exchanges has partly overcome this impediment by permitting a third-party broker to negotiate transfers and set prices and other terms.

Despite its benefits, water marketing, like other "mixed" forms of water management that combine private rights and public infrastructure, has its detractors and critics. As demands for scarce water supplies grow, the price for water is often driven inexorably higher. As a result, so-called "bidding wars" can occur, which leave poorer communities in a position where they are likely to pay more for needed supplies. It can also generate unforeseen environmental impacts on an exporting region: the Salton Sea and Imperial Irrigation district exemplify this problem. Here, an already brackish water supply is being further depleted by threats to sell more water from agricultural districts to San Diego. And there is the unanswerable question of permanence: once sold, can water rights be bought back? Will markets lead to a monopolization of water rights by those with the deepest pockets?

Water marketing can protect equity and environmental quality in basins-of-origin (e.g., mandating return flows, protecting in-stream values, incorporating expiration dates for trades, and the like). It can also help better define the conditions under which water rights are transferred from one party to another. Responsible trading of water is not unlike responsible trading of stocks or agriculture "futures." Various means for ensuring transparency of available supply and the going price for water must be provided to buyers. Allowances must be made for public review of trades. And explicit environmental protection measures such as water banks for trades across state lines, and requirements that a portion of the water remain associated with its previous uses, may also be needed to make trades sustainable.

The Bottled Water Fetish

Amidst all the geopolitical trends regarding the control and consumption of freshwater, the most remarkable has been the growth of the bottled water industry – which has experienced a growth rate in product consumption of some 5–7 percent annually. In 2007, a year for which reliable global statistics are available, more than 200 billion liters (some 55 billion gallons) of bottled water were sold around the world, mostly in North America and Europe. In the US, the total amount sold that year (33 billion liters or approximately 10 billion gallons) averaged out to about 110 liters (or almost 30 gallons) of water per person. This figure was far greater than the per person consumption of milk or beer, and was exceeded only by soft drinks. Per capita consumption in Europe, particularly in Italy and France, is even greater. Consumption has also grown rapidly in the newly emerging market economies of Asia and the Pacific basin.

A major reason for bottled water's rapid growth is that many people believe it to be healthier and safer than tap water. An outbreak of cryptosporidium – most notoriously in Milwaukee, Wisconsin – which made over 400,000 people ill, and resulted in the death of over 100 people in 1993, was a catalytic event that helped propel the bottled water industry into prominence. Even so, health concerns explain only a fraction of the industry's growth – at least among higher-income consumers. Clever marketing has also played an important role, transforming bottled water into an icon of vitality, health, mobility, safety, and fashion. And it is a convenient "grab-and-go" product.

While bottled water is a healthful alternative to unsafe public water supplies in many parts of the world, in developed nations where tap water is stringently regulated – as well as cheap – it is simply not a bona fide, healthful alternative. Moreover, in *all* countries, when the environmental, energy, economic, and potential health impacts from the manufacture and bottling of water are taken into consideration, its health and safety may make it less healthful lower than tap water.

It also poses enormous geopolitical challenges to the sustainability of local water supplies.

For starters, bottled water is largely unregulated in quality, often fails independent tests for purity, and imposes gross impacts on energy and resource use. Moreover, as a public supply source, it is fantastically expensive. By some estimates, bottled water can range upwards of 350 times more in cost than the equivalent unit of tap water. And it is usually not fluoridated – thus posing an indirect hazard to dental hygiene in children.

The production, distribution, and transportation of bottled water generate a huge carbon footprint. Annually, over three million tons of polyethylene terephthalate, or PET, the plastic used to manufacture most water bottles, is produced across the globe, with one-third of that amount produced in the US alone. Production consumes the equivalent of some 50 million barrels of oil, and additional energy is used to treat the water, fill and cap the bottles, and transport them. As the bottled water fetish has grown, the import of water from exotic locales such as Fiji or France, adds distance-to-market transportation, and thus energy consumption. In short, on an average basis, bottled water production and consumption consumes some 2,000 times the amount of energy that goes into delivering tap water – and is thus far more energy intensive.

The potential health and environmental problems bottled water generates are also significant. Ironically, the manufacture of PET bottles consumes freshwater – lots of it (some 17.5 kilograms for each kilogram of PET). And, the manufacturing process generates significant amounts of hazardous air pollutants and other contaminants. In 2004, for instance, Coca-Cola Co. recalled its entire Dasani line of bottled water from the British market after levels of bromate, a potentially harmful chemical, were found to exceed legal standards. In 2007, the Canadian Food Inspection Agency warned the public not to consume imported Jermuk Classic Natural Sparkling Mineral Water because it contained excessive levels of arsenic.

Other contaminants that are commonly found in bottled water include the phthalate DEHP, an ingredient in plastic that the Food and Drug Administration has investigated for some 15 years, and which has been linked to problems with male fertility, obesity, and hormonal imbalance. More disturbing is the fact that while tap water in most countries, including the US, is regulated by national environmental agencies such as the EPA, bottled water is loosely regulated – if it is regulated at all – as a food product. Unlike tap water, the source of bottled water and its known threats do not have to be posted on consumer labels. And, some 88 percent of PET bottles are thrown away and not recycled. When discarded, significant levels of antimony and other toxic chemicals used in the manufacture of PET bottles leach into landfills and, eventually, groundwater.

Geopolitical sustainability and environmental justice concerns are also significant issues. Large multinational corporations, including French firms Evian and Perrier, the latter a subsidiary of the giant Swiss firm Nestlé, have successfully bought up and secured local water rights in many locations across the US and the globe, including the Great Lakes, Florida, Maine, and Texas, to operate high-capacity wells and manufacturing plants. And US soft-drink manufacturers who have entered the lucrative bottled water market have done so by essentially marketing filtered tap water. As a proportion of the world's total supply of freshwater, bottled water use makes an insignificant dent in supply. However, when concentrated in less developed rural areas, the exploitation of springs and aquifers can have devastating local environmental impacts, especially on pristine headwaters, streams, springs, and aquifers. Some reports attribute reductions in local stream flow of upwards of one-half or more.

Instances where local resistance has been successful against corporate powers are rare and infrequent. The community of Wisconsin Dells, Wisconsin, secured a successful – and rare – defeat of Swiss-based Nestlé after the conglomerate announced plans to set up a Perrier bottling plant in the area. In India, both Coca-Cola and PepsiCo – major multinational corporations that bottle water under their own labels – have faced major citizen group opposition due to severe local water shortages prompted by their extraction of surface- and groundwater: entire stretches of rivers such as the Bhavani in the state of Tamil Nadu have been sold to Coca-Cola. Community protests have led a Coca-Cola bottling plant in Plachimada to be shut down in 2005, while a Pepsi plant in Pudusseri, a community suffering from severe freshwater scarcity, had its operating license revoked by the local municipal council. These protests have even been cited at recent G8 meetings, such as that in Evian, France, in the early part of the decade.

While making little actual dent in sales, there has been a distinct, if small cultural shift among well-educated and upper-income consumers toward bottled water and its risks as a result of such issues. This shift has been most visible in Europe and North America, and has even been exploited by water utilities – both public and private – as a means of "re-branding" their product as healthful and even better tasting. Middle-class people are beginning to view the industry, especially in developed countries, as a harbinger of various threats – the commodification of water, its bulk export, its high cost, and its threat to human rights. This is even prompting some bottled water companies to re-think their own marketing strategies and public relations campaigns. Edmonton-based Earth Water, for example, a national bottler of spring and osmosis water, forges an explicit connection between bottled water consumption in affluent nations and the fragility of water supply in developing nations: it donates net profits to the United Nations Refugee Agency, which runs water aid programs.

While concerns regarding bottled water's lack of regulation and environmental impact are growing among the affluent, however, less affluent minority populations markedly prefer its consumption. Moreover, the latter are in some instances being targeted by bottled water companies who exploit their suspicions of tap water safety – a legacy of the fact that many of these groups include recent immigrants from regions in which tap water is demonstrably unsafe; Latin America, for example (table 4.2).

In the US, minority parents are three times more likely to purchase bottled water for their children, even though the non-use of fluoridated tap water may actually result in exposing the children of Latino and other minority groups to greater risks of adverse dental health. It may also subject minorities to tap water filtration scams by disreputable companies that seek to take advantage of vulnerable groups who have had bad experiences with public water supplies in their native countries. Despite widely accepted claims for tap water safety, such experiences only heighten anxiety and suspicion among those who have vivid memories of what it is like to live in fear of the hazards of tap water, and who have good reason not to trust assurances offered by public officials.

Moreover, there are other economic inequities. The watchdog group Corporate Accountability International has identified food-industry giant Nestlé as preying on Latinos in Bronx, New York, by using Spanish television commercials to market a product, "Pure Life," which is actually filtered tap water. Among the unscrupulous claims employed in the advertising is the notion that bottled water can help defeat obesity among Latinos.

An important lesson that emerges from the bottled water phenomenon – as a fetish, fad, and response to fear – is that

Table 4.2   Bottled water use – US perspective

- In *California*, 55 percent of Latinos and 30 percent of whites drink bottled water.
- In *Southern California*, 82 percent of Latinos and 68 percent of whites drink bottled water.
- In 2007, per capita consumption of bottled water in the *United States* was 27.6 gal – a 9.5 percent increase from 2005.
- Average cost of 60 gal of tap water in the US = 13.5 cents; average cost of 60 gal of bottled water = $48.

Table 4.3   The seven sins of bottled water

1. Plastic bottles are made from petroleum.
2. The bottles often go into the trash, rather than the recycle bin (in part because many states don't offer five-cent deposits to encourage recycling, as they do on soda and beer cans and bottles).
3. The water is pumped far from where it is sold, creating needless pollution as trucks and barges transport it across the country or around the world.
4. Some local communities have objected to the sale of their water, arguing that the water underground or flowing from natural springs is publicly owned and should not be exploited for profit.
5. Bottled water is rarely as closely monitored as tap water.
6. Tap water in the United States, when provided by a municipal system, is the most highly monitored and safe supply in the world.
7. Fifty percent of the water sold in little plastic bottles is tap water, but it costs an awful lot more per gallon.

the public's perception of freshwater control and its implications is complex. Bottled water is expensive, probably
unsustainable, and of questionable health value. However, it
is not just a "lifestyle" commodity of the well-to-do. It is also a
product attractive to the less affluent who distrust, and often
have little confidence in, the institutions that manage tap
water (table 4.3). This fact underscores the need to reform all

large water provision systems – whether publically or privately managed.[12]

Challenges Facing Providers

As we have seen, freshwater providers – whether they sell and market their product through a publically owned utility or a private, stockholder-owned company – are, in reality, "mixed" enterprises. They obtain their product through government-owned and controlled "wholesale" distribution systems. These systems consist of publically constructed dams and reservoirs, aqueducts, and management agencies including river basin commissions or groundwater management bureaus – the types of entities we discussed in chapter 3.

Further, as mixed enterprises subject to both market demand and public expectations to provide reliable, efficient service, they are also subject to criticism regarding how fairly, equitably, and sustainably they allocate freshwater. While private vendors have been frequently criticized for not considering freshwater a basic human right, and for limiting public access to decisions, so-called public providers are subject to the charge that they do not always exercise optimal stewardship: they are sometimes less than vigilant in averting water losses, and fail to cooperate on a regional basis with other providers for political reasons.

The revolution in freshwater consumerism exemplified by the bottled water phenomenon adds a further wrinkle to the "mixed" nature of freshwater provision, and to the problems of fairness and sustainability. By transforming freshwater into an expensive, resource-intensive product that uses vast amounts of energy and generates hazardous wastes, bottled water is not very environmentally friendly. Its "manufacture" and use, moreover, raise equity issues in two ways. First, because bottled water vendors try to acquire exclusive water rights in communities adjacent to sources of water, they antagonize less powerful groups. Second, overt marketing of bottled water to vulnerable minority groups, sometimes falsely enticed to buy their product for fear that tap water is impure or unhealthful, is a form of economic exploitation. I suggest that all three of these challenges: the mixed nature of the water provision business, the equity and sustainability of these businesses' operations, and the emergence of bottled water as a new form of freshwater consumerism, are forcing us to reconsider the importance of transparency, equity, and stewardship in the geopolitics of freshwater.

Oftentimes, discussions of private-versus-public water ownership pay insufficient attention to an important operational complaint common to both types of provider: their frequent lack of transparency. By transparency, we mean that what they do, and how they do it, must be open to public scrutiny, and be clearly articulated and understandable. Simply because a vendor is in business to turn a profit does not mean that it has to be opaque or secretive. Likewise, the fact that a vendor may be a "public" utility operating in a democratic society does not ensure it will always operate openly.

Careful examination of the process by which private vendors acquire the right to provide freshwater to cities, towns, and rural districts in Africa, Asia, and Latin America suggests that transparency is often problematical. Generally, the competitive bidding process under which local governments choose vendors features a high level of transparency. Companies are required to provide detailed documentation featuring technical, financial, and legal information about their operations, engineering expertise, and how they intend to satisfy water demands if they are selected. In short, the information they are required to provide is not too dissimilar from what public water providers in advanced industrial nations commonly provide to their customers.

However, when negotiating with less developed countries, private vendors often lack transparency in three respects. First, they usually say very little about how they intend to serve low-income residents. Second, they are rarely required to provide – nor do they voluntarily make available – detailed assessments of water infrastructure leading, once they obtain contracts, to "re-bidding" of important features of their agreements. And third, they commonly under-bid their competition (a practice called "dive-bidding") in order to acquire contracts that, once consummated, can be renegotiated – a process made easier if the government with whom one is negotiating is weak, or relies on external consultants in its negotiations.

A well-documented example is Manila, Philippines. In the early 2000s, two concessions – one in East and the other in West Manila – were let by the Philippine government. While both winning bids were well below their nearest competitors by wide margins, a fact that should have alerted negotiators' suspicions, the consultants who reviewed the bids failed to be more vigilant. Once the bids were let and the companies began operations, neither could deliver on its promise to provide adequate service. Both asked to renegotiate terms of their contracts, and were allowed to increase the rates they charged consumers: in effect passing on the costs of their initial low bids to water users.

There are three lessons from the Manila case regarding transparency that are relevant to all providers. First, under-bidding and false or misleading operational promises are most likely to arise whenever water and sanitation are in dire need of improvement – a condition common in many poorer countries. In such a situation, consumers and governments often lack the ability to sufficiently pose the right questions and conduct full and complete economic analyses. Second, such problems are worsened when the process of privatization is hurried, and vendors are unfamiliar with local conditions. This was clearly the case in Manila. And third, where local governance is weak, again as in many developing countries, local stakeholders including the urban poor see their interests overlooked or ignored. In short, transparency requires a strong, vital, and robust public sector to provide regulation and ensure accountability. We find such conditions in much of Europe, for example, where private vendors provide water services, but where public organizations provide oversight and encourage broad participation. This is not often the case in developing nations where privatization is vertically integrated and poorly regulated – as in the Philippines case.

Fairness

As we have seen, there are almost as many ways to define fairness in regards to freshwater provision as there are freshwater users. In general, fairness means that a sufficient supply of clean, potable freshwater is provided to users at an affordable price. But what do we mean by the terms "sufficient supply" and "affordable"? Is it obvious we can all agree on their meaning? Defenders of privatization often point out how critics wrongly charge them with violating fundamental human rights for freshwater by seeking "full cost-recovery through user fees." In short, the effort to earn a profit through providing such essential services as freshwater supply and treatment is seen as morally wrong because it inherently conflicts with the basic needs of the poor. Moreover, this profit is often seen as accruing to multinational corporations based in the wealthiest countries, while the poorest countries pay the user fees. Closer examination reveals that corporations do not act – nor benefit – alone. Politicians concerned with re-election may impede implementation of progressive pricing policies that shift the burden of paying for new water systems from the poor to the middle class or businesses out of fear of losing votes in the next election. Moreover, private vendors often do not fully recover all their costs.

In thinking through this moral argument, it is important to realize that its truth lies more in *how* privatization is implemented as opposed to the fact of privatization itself. As we have seen, one can have privately owned retail water provision that is both politically accountable and a good service provider, if certain conditions are met. The advent of privatization in China in the last 30 years illustrates the possibilities, as well as challenges in meeting these conditions.

Dalian, a port city located at the southern end of the Liaodong Peninsula in northeastern China, has experienced phenomenal economic and population growth since the 1980s. Much of this growth was propelled by efforts begun in 1984, under Deng Xiaoping, to modernize the country. Dalian was one of several municipalities declared an "open" coastal city and given considerable autonomy in its economic planning, including becoming one of the first Chinese cities to encourage free trade zones and foreign trade. The Dalian Economic and Technology Development Zone, established in 1988, became one of China's most successful enterprise zones.

By the early 1990s, however, water shortages became a serious impediment to the city's economic growth. Many areas of the municipal region received water service for only a few hours a day. Moreover, frequent service disruptions had major public health implications, including contaminated water supplies and inadequate wastewater treatment. The Dalian Water Supply Project, begun in the mid-1990s, provided new infrastructure to address these shortages and meet increasing demand. Large segments of this project were "privatized," with for-profit vendors providing infrastructure improvements and enhanced treatment capacity. To cover the large cost increases associated with these improvements, water tariffs were also increased dramatically, from 1995 to 2001, at an average annual rate of 12.8 percent. This was declared necessary in order to finance the improvements while retaining the enterprise zone's credit rating.[13]

The project achieved its objectives. All the new facilities to provide additional water and water treatment operate well, and there has been a phenomenal growth in residential water connections in Dalian, far in excess of expectations, as residents hooked up to the municipal provision system rather than continuing to rely on local wells and other intermittent supplies. The project also increased water supply to commerce and industry, removing potential constraints to economic expansion and improving business investment and employment throughout the region.

There are two important lessons of this project for equity. First, the rate increases and privatization of supplies were both introduced gradually, and while annual rate increases were high, they were not unreasonable given rising average annual incomes. Second, the rate increases went directly into increased investments that served the beneficial purpose of ensuring an adequate long-term, safe, and secure freshwater supply. Local consumers accepted the higher tariffs in part because they became readily convinced that services would become more adequate and reliable, thus leading to an improved way-of-life.

This is consistent with the experiences of other developing nations with privatization which show how its introduction must actually address underlying problems of water and sanitation provision to be viewed as acceptable. It is probably also true that, in China, privatization was more readily accepted because it was not tied (and the government would not allow it to be tied) to international private sector participation or development assistance.[14]

Stewardship

Most legitimate water providers, regardless of whether they are privately or publically owned, pride themselves on seeking to provide safe, pure water supplies to their customers. While they may, on occasion, fail, it is rarely for want of trying. By contrast, in many developing nations, where public supplies are provided by modest, informal vendors, rudimentary treatment methods are applied to freshwater, often resulting in supplies of questionable quality. Ironically, this fact, coupled with the fiscal constraints facing government efforts to provide reliable, safe, and secure supplies, is what gives rise to the impulse to privatize freshwater provision. The quest to be good stewards over the quality of public water supplies is a strong aspiration. The cost of its achievement is what makes it an elusive goal.

Where stewardship intentions are more often put to the test is in environmental sustainability. Here, governments are as often to blame as are private enterprises for failure. As we have seen, most provision systems are "mixed," with the state providing dams, reservoirs, diversion systems, and other "plumbing" to move water over vast distances. The result, as we saw in chapters 2 and 3, is environmental degradation in the name of water resources development.

Here too, however, innovations such as water marketing can be employed to transform elaborate water distribution systems into vehicles for restoring environmental amenities. This can be achieved by selling or leasing water rights to environmental groups and other benefactors who will ensure that water supplies are left in rivers and streams to benefit fish and wildlife as well as cities, farms, and ranches. From a geopolitical standpoint, such schemes afford the kind of informal, ad hoc collaboration which advocates of so-called "social-ecological" systems have long heralded – a means to negotiate agreements to govern water through sharing information as well as water.[15] In chapter 5, we consider the deeper implications of such agreements and the ways amicably negotiated remedies can only be reached if cooperation leads to equality among all water users.

CHAPTER FIVE

Water Ethics and
Environmental Justice

Underlying the geopolitics of freshwater are two facts that are hard to refute: achieving sustainability requires international cooperation; and getting parties to cooperate requires that they trust the justness of what they are agreeing to. Perhaps few countries are as familiar with these facts as Pakistan and India. Both are at loggerheads over the latter's plans to construct a large hydropower project on the Kishanganga-Neelum River – a tributary of the Jhelum. Some Pakistanis fear the dam would give India power to manipulate the river's flow to the detriment of Pakistan's agriculture, an activity which employs nearly half the country's population.

In fall 2011, the Netherlands-based International Court of Arbitration unanimously issued a "stay order" on the dam's construction. The court did not actually rule in favor of either country. However, mindful that both are building large dams in the same basin – the Kishanganga Hydroelectric Project, being built by India, is scheduled for completion in 2014, while Pakistan's Neelum-Jhelum Hydroelectric Project is to be finished in 2016 – it wanted time to consider the merits of each nation's case.

Behind the court's delaying action is the 1960 Indus Water Treaty, negotiated by both nations, which contains a principle known in international law as the "priority rights method." This principle accords rights to permanently alter a river to whichever country's engineering plans are closer to completion. Ironically, although Pakistan won the current "stay,"

India's Kishanganga project is closer to being finished. Whatever the court finally decides, two things are certain. First, each party would like the court to approve its plans so as to accord them legal and moral legitimacy. And second, while Pakistan initiated the litigation, India agreed to submit itself to the court – suggesting it agrees with the justness of the process, if not necessarily the ultimate outcome.[1]

This case – as with many others we have discussed – underscores the fact that, with few exceptions, activities that pollute, deplete, or harness freshwater, or cause it to become more costly or flood ravaged, do not respect territorial boundaries. Moreover, such activities raise questions about who benefits, who loses, and what's fair. As we recall from chapter 2, water shortages in one nation may encourage refugees to seek food in others. It also may encourage countries to impound rivers neighboring countries depend on. And, as we saw in chapter 3 in cases from Europe, Russia, Australia, and Asia, farming, manufacturing, diversion, over-fishing, and climate change pose threats far beyond a single locale. Finally, as chapter 4 showed, disputes over water provision in London, La Paz, or Manila are often caused by investment decisions made by corporate boards hundreds or even thousands of miles away.

In this chapter we discuss how international cooperation on amicable remedies to alleviate freshwater scarcity, unequal access, river development, and pollution must be based on equality, transparency, and fairness. We begin by examining how water disputes revolve around what people consider just – and not just political control or money. We also consider how access to freshwater, many think, is a basic human right. We then weigh the ethical implications of three potential, and non-conventional, remedies to global freshwater problems: conservation, wastewater re-use, and desalination. Throughout, we argue that global reform requires that experts and officials take seriously calls for an ethical water policy that transcends national boundaries.

Justice and Global Norms

Conflicts over the ways we control freshwater are often the result of ethical differences. In like manner, proposed remedies for how to sustainably manage freshwater employ ethical justifications on behalf of their adoption. Ethics are widely-shared, but wide-ranging and varied values based on moral or spiritual principles. As regards freshwater, these principles embrace beliefs regarding: *how* freshwater should be allocated; *who* should participate in decisions regarding allocation and quality; *what* constitutes proper consideration toward other species' needs; and whether people have a *right* to a certain amount and quality of freshwater.

Neither environmental philosophers nor water policy officials fully agree on what makes a water policy ethical. Nonetheless, there is surprisingly widespread accord regarding what sorts of things make it *unethical*. For instance, a policy which grants access to high-quality freshwater only to a few, while ignoring the needs of the many, would be considered *unjust*. Similarly, actions which fail to protect the freshwater needs of plants and animals would also be considered wrong, if for no other reason than harm to them usually affects people. And decisions regarding freshwater made without the benefit of broad representation of those directly affected by them – in other words, without democratic consultation – are also considered unethical.[2] Agreement on these and other principles of *environmental justice* has practical importance, as we will see.

Beyond these broad principles are two distinct aspects of environmental justice which are also pertinent to global freshwater management – and for which there also tends to be widespread agreement. First, the management of water affects people and other species in different ways. Certain groups – as well as some species – are more prone to harms associated with the geopolitics of water than are others. As we saw in chapter 1, for example, the very old and very young are especially vulnerable to water-borne contaminants and illnesses. Moreover, as noted in chapters 2 and 3, some non-human species are more sensitive to fluctuations of in-stream flow or pollutant exposure than others. And, as we discussed in chapter 4, the poor are more vulnerable than the wealthy to privately supplied water sources priced out of the former's reach.

Second, because the impacts and burdens of freshwater decisions affect people and other species differently, and because needs for clean, plentiful water also vary, decision-making *processes* are as critical to achieving environmental justice as are decisional *outcomes*. In short, if decisions regarding freshwater could result in people suffering undue harm or indignity to their health and well-being, or placed at risk by contaminated, degraded, or depleted water, then it is important that these decisions include their voices, as well as those of others deemed relevant. The latter could include future generations whose needs and interests will be affected by decisions made today. These are lofty goals. Can they be achieved through international agreement?

While there is wide consensus over what makes control, management, and allocation of freshwater unjust, there's far less *political* agreement over how ethical norms should be applied to its management through law, regulation, and policy. This is especially the case in regards to international disputes over freshwater caused by competition over the development of shared rivers, or contention over who is responsible for dumping wastes into a boundary watershed. The India-Pakistan conflict cited at the beginning of this chapter underscores this fact, as does chapter 3's case studies of the Danube and Rhine basins, for instance. In recent decades, there have been many international debates over how to manage the quality and supply of freshwater in ways that protect the least well-off, while at the same time promoting economic development – two important elements of freshwater sustainability.

The goal of environmental justice has been articulated in the United Nations' International Hydrological Program writings on water ethics, for example. These pronouncements allude to various "victims" of water crises, such as women, the very young, and the frail, the destitute, and national minorities. Moreover, the Dublin Principles of 1992 – an oft-cited international statement – explicitly recognizes the role of women in managing water, as well as everyone's fundamental right to water.

There are two major challenges in applying this goal of environmental justice to global freshwater policy. The first is lack of agreement among nation-states regarding how to translate – or actually implement – a set of codified international principles. As one scholar has noted "there is little evidence of a common normative structure in the form of interstate cooperation [that] has taken across the world's shared river basins, and there is no compelling evidence that international legal principles are taking on greater depth of meaning or even moving in an identifiable direction."[3]

The second challenge is more conceptual. Most environmental justice claims with regard to water advance the goal of equity – treating people and nature fairly, and regarding their interests impartially. This notion of equity is one of the reasons countries can agree to try to arbitrate at least some of their differences in international courts, for example, as India and Pakistan are currently doing. Beyond this shared goal, however, there is considerable debate regarding what being fair and impartial means in any particular case. Historically, three approaches have been generally employed to advance this elusive goal: covenants, categorical imperatives, and environmental stewardship.

Covenants began some 5,000 years ago in the Middle East and were applied to environmental as well as social policies. The Hebrew Torah and official records from ancient Assyria and Sumeria cite their use and their basis upon three principles. First, when people benefit from land and water resources, they implicitly agree to manage them responsibly, and with regard for the welfare of future generations. Second, such implicit agreement is permanent – it cannot be broken. And third, these agreements derive their moral authority from being universally endorsed.

A modern example of a global "covenant" for environmental justice and water is the 1948 Universal Declaration of Human Rights, promulgated by the UN General Assembly in a period of post-war optimism. The declaration enshrined two important principles: (1) the right to marry and have a family and (2) "(e)veryone has the right to a standard of living adequate for the health and well-being of himself and of his family," including food, *water*, clothing, housing and medical care. The Universal Declaration was intended as a "proclamation" of the General Assembly to serve as a "common standard of achievement for all peoples and all nations" which should "strive by teaching and education to promote respect for these rights and freedoms and by progressive measures, national and international, to secure their universal and effective recognition and observance, and to promote general welfare."[4]

The categorical imperative, identified with the German philosopher Immanuel Kant, posits that a moral decision should not advance our own happiness but be generalizable to all who face a similar situation. Kant was mainly interested in ethical relationships among people. Nonetheless, because his ideas were partly a response to the dominant utilitarian views of his contemporaries, they are relevant to environmental justice and water. In practical terms, Kant was really asking us to "do unto others as we would have them do unto us."

An instructive water policy example is the (US) Wild and Scenic Rivers Act, which explicitly promotes the idea of "compensation" for previous losses of streams that were deemed historically significant. It embraces the principle that the "established national policy of dam(s) must be complemented by preserving other . . . selected rivers" and avoiding significant future harm to them through adopting a uniform national policy. In contrast to covenants, categorical imperatives stress respect for prior promises and commitments; not merely promoting general welfare. Stewardship further embraces the idea that resources are neither inherited nor owned, but "borrowed" by the present generation from future ones. A healthy environment is characterized by integrity and stability, and we should view ourselves as a part of all creation – and not apart from it. In short: all living things have inherent value.[5]

Stewardship owes its origins to a variety of ethical doctrines. At its center is the notion that humans are responsible for caring for the natural environment – a view shared by traditions ranging from *pragmatic conservation* during the nineteeth century to contemporary religious views toward ecology. Advocates of the "progressive conservationist" tradition understood humanity's obligation to care for nature to be rooted in the unique stature of people as creatures of reason, and who have a capacity to serve as caretakers and guardians of natural resources. The post-World War II conservationist Aldo Leopold added an important and highly regarded stricture to this notion: in caring for resources, including freshwater, we should also show care for our own welfare and be fully cognizant of nature's limits. As he stated: "A thing is right if . . . it preserves the integrity, stability, and beauty of the biosphere."

An example applied to freshwater management is the (US) Endangered Species Act which bars federal agencies from actions that jeopardize freshwater resources or impair habitat. The act is replete with stewardship principles, as in these passages which state: "various species of fish, wildlife, and plants in the US have been rendered extinct as a consequence of economic growth and development un-tempered by adequate concern and conservation," while others "have been so depleted in numbers that they are in danger of or threatened with extinction." These species have "esthetic, ecological, educational, historical, recreational, and scientific value" and we, "as a sovereign state in the international community [must] conserve" these threatened species. "Conservation," moreover, means employing "all methods and procedures which are necessary to bring any endangered species or threatened species to the point at which the measures provided pursuant to this Act are no longer necessary."[6]

While these three approaches to environmental justice are by no means exhaustive, they illustrate the range of ethical challenges facing freshwater management. They also underscore the fact that water disputes probably cannot be resolved through any approach that favors one group's notion of fairness or impartiality at the expense of another group's perception of what constitutes a hardship or unfair burden. Moreover, no approach can ignore the water needs of plants and animals, or those for human health, and fully embrace equity. For these reasons, we cannot escape the necessity for an environmentally just *process* for reconciling different ethical claims.

In addition to long-standing debate over equity, there is more recent interest in the notion of water as a fundamental human right. A number of international initiatives supported by non-governmental advocacy groups insist that all people possess basic rights to vital resources, including freshwater.

> **Table 5.1   UNESCO Commission on Ethics and Scientific Knowledge**
>
> 1. *Human dignity*: Water is a basic human right.
> 2. *Participation*: Citizen participation in decision-making regarding water.
> 3. *Solidarity*: We all rely on, and depend upon ecosystems that are linked up- and downstream by water.
> 4. *Common good*: Water is essential to the full realization of human potential and capacity.
> 5. *Stewardship*: We need an ethic that balances using, changing, modifying, and preserving our land and water resources.

Access to these resources, they contend, is as fundamental to human dignity as are traditional civil liberties enshrined in national constitutions which guarantee freedom of speech, press, non-verbal expression, peaceable protest, and the practice of religious faith. Among international initiatives advocating this view is UNESCO's World Commission on Ethics of Scientific Knowledge and Technology (2002) which articulates a set of ethical principles toward water (table 5.1) predicated on the notion that access to water is a basic human right.

Such initiatives try to do more than merely articulate claims for water as a human right – they also seek to enshrine this right-to-water into international law and to achieve global consensus regarding access to potable freshwater as a cornerstone of environmental justice. Water as human right initiatives tend to fall into one of three approaches: "needs equals rights," "indigenous peoples' inclusion," and "protection of vulnerable populations." While all three should be viewed as complementary – not mutually exclusive – initiatives, each emphasizes particularly unique policy problems.

The "needs equals rights" approach is exemplified by the 2009 World Water Forum held in Istanbul, in which the

International Union for the Conservation of Nature (IUCN) strongly vocalized its concern with freshwater privatization. Projecting a world water crisis caused by drought, growing demands, and problems of affordability, IUCN charged corporate water vendors with exploiting the misfortunes of poorer countries and their economically disadvantaged citizens. By transforming water into a commodity that profit-oriented private concerns can trade in, IUCN's fear – expressed at the Istanbul meeting – is that private ownership converts water from a basic right to a privilege controlled by those wealthy enough to leverage its availability, benefit by its higher cost (which makes it a worthwhile investment), and who can acquire access to its control. The only viable alternative to this transformation, critics argue, is to ensure that the right to freshwater is enshrined through "ownership" by all citizens by means of public control and oversight. This ownership will guarantee both access and affordability.

"Indigenous peoples' inclusion" is a novel and somewhat more recent approach to water rights. Its premise is that while many people are disadvantaged by lack of potable water, indigenous people living in isolated, rural districts in developing nations are often the most disadvantaged of all because they are already marginalized from the levers of power. Moreover, the impacts of climate and other global environmental change discussed in chapters 1 and 2 are far more likely to adversely impact these groups' access to freshwater than others. This is because the lands on which these indigenous peoples reside are likely to be lost to development as more prosperous, powerful groups covet their forests, minerals, and watersheds. Recognizing this threat, NGOs such as Survival International are vigorously advocating protections of indigenous peoples' water rights under the UN Declaration on the Rights of Indigenous Peoples. Survival International advocates greater protection to indigenous populations through measures to ensure their continuing right to ownership of their native lands; protection of their legal right to give or withhold consent to development; and furthering their right to be consulted with regards to their unique knowledge about local water resources when allocation decisions are made. A critical equity-related issue regarding indigenous rights is the potential for conflict between the "common good" notion of rights held by many indigenous peoples in contrast to the individual property-based concepts of water rights held in more modern polities. We will return to this point momentarily.

The "vulnerable populations" argument is really a variant of the indigenous rights approach – broadened to include the poor, ethnically disadvantaged, and future generations. Vulnerability is taken to mean extreme liability to the ways water is managed. While shortages of potable water and threats to public health from pollution are considered important, so too are the social disparities that arise via construction of large dams, for instance. In recent years, advocates of this approach include Oxfam and International Rivers Network, which both focus on pollution and public health-related issues, while the World Commission on Dams and other entities tend to highlight the disparities generated by large impoundments which cause population dislocation and loss of ancestral lands (e.g., Three Gorges Dam discussed in chapter 3) while conferring benefits to others in the form of flood control, electrical power, and water supply.

The language of "human rights" is frequently invoked in international forums in an attempt to identify a humane basis for resolving water problems that transcends the interests of particular individuals, groups, or countries. This makes it a familiar, global vernacular. Nevertheless, it is hardly a language without problems. As some critics rightly point out, as with many languages, *human rights* has different "dialects," some with decided limitations. In the US, for example, "rights talk" has been criticized for "tend[ing] to be presented as absolute, individual, and independent of any necessary relation to responsibilities," in contrast to rights language in other liberal democracies which emphasize *duties* to others and respect for diversity of needs. Ambiguities that accompany such diversity may cause people to talk past each other or even invite deliberate stalemate. While one party may characterize a dispute over water privatization as outrage over excessive charges that discriminate against the rights of the poor to water, for example, another might describe the nub of the conflict to be a corporate water vendor's *property* right to charge a fair price for service rendered.

Human rights arguments are also limited in their ethical legitimacy by over-emphasis on the use of power to achieve supposedly just ends. As one recent forum on the ethics of freshwater concluded, "history reveals that where there is power, there is potential for as much mischief as good." This is because human rights principles are as subject to distortion and manipulation as any beliefs known to humankind. Practical examples of this criticism are recent cases regarding water and property rights in South America. As we noted earlier, many indigenous cultures practice a form of communal rights with regards to water. Territorial "rights" to land and other resources are often viewed as held in common by members of an ethnic group occupying a given territory. Thus, rights of access to freshwater, for example, are seen as bestowing the rights for all group members to use, but are not within the province of anyone to appropriate. In parts of Latin America – particularly the Andean region, Amazon basin, and parts of Central America – this has sometimes led to contention between peasants and the state over both the subdivision of land, and the appropriation of freshwater. Indigenous groups have lobbied the Inter-American Commission on Human Rights in an effort to clarify how both systems of "rights," properly understood, might be better reconciled in order to allow indigenous peoples continued access to use, enjoy, and benefit from water and other natural resources even if their ancestral lands are "sold" by the state to, say, large corporations for development.

Passionate affirmations based on human rights arguments still reverberate throughout the world. Perhaps because they link regional cultures to international values through regional rights languages, they have inspired meaningful change in Asia, Africa, South America, Europe, and the United States over the last 60 years. Nonetheless, to the extent they are embedded in linguistic, conceptual, and definitional debates, their application remains subject to criticism and – important for the cause of water and environmental justice – to self-criticism. The rights-based exercise of power over water must be held accountable to other standards that both transcend and inform understandings of the rights that legitimate that power. To the extent that a claim upon "rights" engenders a certain claim upon political or economic power, for example, then the greater the need for other resources to at least check distorted applications of human rights, helping in turn to refine, sharpen, and strengthen their application.[7] These debates – over equity and human rights – can be seen in discussions of the fairness of innovations to conserve water.

Are Conservation Innovations Fair?

In response to the challenges of *population growth*, continued *urbanization*, and *climate variability and change*, public officials and corporate entities the world over are implementing a variety of policy innovations to re-allocate, conserve, re-use, recycle, and otherwise expand the availability of freshwater. Innovations intended to conserve or use less water, or to encourage ways of using water more efficiently (i.e., using less water to meet the same needs) are referred to as *demand-side methods*. They include variable rate systems that charge more for greater volumes of water use; and mandatory water appliance retrofitting or other conservation measures. These may be coupled with direct metering of households where demand is measured at the point of consumer use. Because these innovations are still novel, they afford an important means to explore ethical challenges with regards to control of the world's water.

Demand-side approaches may burden economically disadvantaged groups by ignoring their ability to pay for freshwater supplies, forcing them to adopt and install high-efficiency – and higher cost water savings appliances, and contemporary innovations intended to better manage our planet's freshwater and to avert shortages.

In the nation-sized state of California, where metering experience has been cited as having international application, water savings of between 20 and 40 percent have been documented. Metering's environmental justice impacts vary, however. International accounts are useful for comparison. Recall in chapter 4, how the introduction of metering in Salta Province, Argentina, led to protests, vandalism, and refusal to accept meters. This was prompted by its introduction at the same time aggressive enforcement of bill payment, increasing block rate prices, and household charges for meter installation began. These actions were also prompted by widespread fears that meters would not be accurately read and residents would be charged for excess water usage.

In Europe, by contrast, studies show that metering has been embraced by the public as a fair means to increase both reliability (i.e. making leak detection easier) and water conservation. One reason appears to be the different role played by privatization. While in Argentina, as in many developing nations, privatization is viewed as an effort to commodify water and vertically integrate services, in much of Europe by contrast, privatization of water services is kept distinct from planning, control, and regulation, with oversight reserved to public organizations including river basin authorities.

Increasing bloc rate (IBR) pricing charges customers more per unit of water used once their volume of use exceeds an average-derived use level (a "conservation base"). In principle, IBR assumes that the greater one's income, the greater one's water use – an assumption that is probably valid when applied to homeowners who practice widespread outdoor use (e.g. landscaping, pools). Thus, it appears to be equitable as well as efficient: when introduced, water savings of between 10 and 15 percent have been reported. Aside from ability-to-pay issues, however, IBR may create a political conundrum for public utilities whose elected boards will be held to account by voters for unpopular rate increases. Anecdotal evidence suggests that such elected boards often prefer voluntary as opposed to mandatory measures to conserve water.

Another criticism of IBR is that it is not always practiced in areas that need it the most. Again, in California where IBR experience is long-standing, two-thirds of the population of the state's southern coastal area pays IBR, and other conservation incentives are also fostered by the region's Metropolitan Water District including encouraging customers to install water efficient appliances and to plant drought-resistant landscapes. Overall, the southern coastal area used nearly 450,000 acre-feet less water in 2005 than a decade earlier, despite having two million additional residents. By contrast, however, many of the more arid, warmer, and desert-like areas of the state's so-called "Inland Empire" do not practice IBR as intensively, if at all.

Some 50–60 percent of residential water use in these inland areas is for landscaping, while indoor use has also risen with single family home ownership – both trends have been accompanied by growth in household incomes. Ironically, however, most communities in this region do not employ IBR but use uniform rates that charge the same amount per gallon. Moreover, for aesthetic reasons, some communities forbid measures that conserve water through, for example, removing lawns and replacing them with water-saving landscaping. The good news is that, statewide, IBR, appliance retrofitting, landscape irrigation improvements, and agricultural conservation in California have reduced water use. In 1980 the state had 23 million people and used some 34 million acre-feet of water. By 2001, the state's 41 million people used 42 million acre-feet. The less sanguine news is that some elements of conservation, such as IBR, have not been borne equally by all regions.[8]

There is little agreement regarding what makes variable water rates and other water conservation innovations fair and equitable. What makes this debate especially problematical is not only the varying ways equity is defined, as we have seen, but because of the compelling debates offered up by the "water as human rights" approach. If, as many human rights groups contend, water should be provided to people regardless of their ability to pay, in accord with what their needs dictate, then defending variable rates is always going to be difficult without agreement over how to define need, ability to pay, and the processes that determine both.

Some water policy experts have attempted to resolve this problem by approaching the general topic of water use, conservation, and fairness of conservation measures from the standpoint of affordability and hardship. Simply stated, do low- and fixed-income households sacrifice other needs in order to pay for water? And if so, are there public policies available to compensate them for this added expense? Furthermore, assuming, as we discussed in chapter 4, that both public and privately owned water providers must garner a sufficient income through their water services in order to deliver reliable, safe, and healthful supplies, would their customers be exposed to greater health risks if these providers received lower revenues?

Anecdotal evidence suggests, as we have seen in earlier chapters, that provision of freshwater already constitutes a burden in many developing countries relative to what people earn. For example, international data indicate that poorer nations use far less water per capita than do highly developed societies – the US as a whole and developing societies' rates of use differ by from three to over ten times. Moreover, within the US alone, per capita usage rates among states and communities, controlling for income, are narrower but similarly discernible, and studies show that many low-income customers face consistent difficulty meeting one or more basic needs, including paying for water. This further suggests that variable conservation rate charges and similar strategies would impose further burdens unless compensating measures were adopted such as sliding-income scales for low-income customers and free leak repairs. Fortunately, many water utilities in developed nations have adopted such measures. Unfortunately, they have not been nearly as widely adopted in developing ones.

There is a further factor that must be considered when drawing conclusions regarding conservation and equity – a *process* issue – public acceptability. Returning to California for a moment, where much of the activity promoting IBR and variable rates has occurred, equity issues have been raised by rate payers in communities in the southern part of the state. These issues mostly take the form of concern for *equal and fair treatment*. For example, customers frequently question how individual household budgets eligible for "conservation" rates are calculated, express skepticism regarding whether increased rates are truly revenue neutral or are a means for public and private vendors to increase their revenue streams, ask whether customers are rewarded for efforts to conserve, and question whether freshwater conservation really has the environmental benefits to fisheries through reducing water imports as is claimed.[9]

From the standpoint of *policy outcome*, it seems clear that some who are asked to pay more for using more water really are economically burdened. Their water use may not be a function of income or lifestyle, but may instead be prompted by factors over which they have little control, special health needs, or the need to care for small children or elderly. For them, added costs truly are a hardship. From the standpoint of *policy process*, however, experience would also suggest that many, regardless of income or ability to pay, may view variable rates as unfair and inequitable if the reasons for the higher rates are not seen as fully justified or justifiable. Both are important policy cautions for those who would adopt such remedies in order to stretch shrinking supplies of freshwater.

Risks of Re-claimed Wastewater and Desalination

Recycled wastewater use presents several environmental justice challenges. It can reduce needs for imported freshwater, thereby alleviating pressures on supplies that would otherwise be diverted from the territory of others, and it reduces wastewater-generated pollution by alleviating the need to dispose of contaminated water in rivers and streams. In considering whether the use of recycled water is fair, however, it is important to acknowledge three concerns. The first is the so-called "toilet-to-tap" issue: the perception that people are being asked to use water that has been diverted from the wastewater stream and practically immediately used as tap water. A second environmental justice issue is that reliance on recycled wastewater to enhance and recharge groundwater supplies and for prescribed potable and non-potable uses may encourage additional growth in water demands thus serving, in effect, as a subsidy for additional residential, commercial, and industrial growth. And third, while a number of studies indicate that potable re-use is safe, doubts have arisen over safeguards.

Important to the environmental justice debate is that perceptions of safety are associated with a sense of inclusion in decision making. In less affluent areas, for those communities suffering from ongoing water-related environmental legacy issues (e.g. abandoned hazardous waste sites, contaminated aquifers), proposals for re-use arouse suspicion and widespread mistrust – even though there is no evidence that these communities are targeted for re-use.

Desalination produces a different set of equity challenges – one that most closely mirrors the stewardship approach mentioned earlier. On the one hand, it remains an expensive, energy-intensive, environmentally risky option that requires some amount of public or taxpayer subsidy to operate profitably. On the other, given that virtually every option for expanding freshwater supply, as opposed to reducing its demand, entails some environmental risk and imposes an economic burden on someone, one must be cautious about applying criticisms to desalination that we would not be willing to apply to other options.

While long used on ships at sea and more especially on nuclear-powered vessels – applications that prove its technical viability – on a domestic scale, desalination embraces a broad set of complex processes that remove salt and other minerals from seawater, brackish water, river water, wastewater, and even treated municipal supplies. Over 12,000 desalination plants in 120 countries currently provide some 14 million m^3 of freshwater daily – an amount still less than 1 percent of the world's total freshwater consumption. Because large-scale desalination uses large amounts of energy, it is very costly, especially when compared to the use of freshwater from streams or aquifers – from $1,000 to $2,200 per acre-foot, compared to $200 an acre-foot for water from conventional supply sources. This is the principal reason that 75 percent of the world's entire desalination capacity is found in the Middle East (mainly Saudi Arabia, Kuwait, Qatar, Bahrain, and the United Arab Emirates). The latter is home to the planet's single largest desalination facility – the Jebel Ali Desalination Plant – Phase 2.

Despite the thus far limited application and use of desalination, there may be some very logical reasons to resort to desalination in certain applications. One reason may be the lack of alternatives. This is the case in the Persian Gulf, Africa, and even portions of the US. Another reason is that, even without the need for additional water supplies, desalination in certain locales is both a necessary and appropriate remediation tool for restoring water quality. Some 30 percent of the world's irrigated areas suffer from some form of salinity problems as a result of dissolved minerals settling on soils, and flowing as runoff into streams and rivers, and desalination plants – including one in Yuma, Arizona, have been built precisely to restore this runoff to a quality sufficient to be used on crops. Thirdly, as the technology improves and demand increases, costs are likely to fall – a trend already occurring in places such as the Middle East.[10]

Wastewater re-use faces adverse perceptions regarding its perceived benefits and risks. The way advocates address these perceptions is critical to its acceptability and perceived fairness. The ability to frame messages about the technology's benefits and risks, and to consult relevant stakeholders, directly affects these perceptions. Again, the experiences of California are instructive, because of the pioneering efforts made in that state to pursue potable wastewater re-use on a large scale – efforts that continue to garner international media attention.

In the 1970s California's Orange County Water District (OCWD) built a wastewater purifying plant – WF 21, a reverse osmosis facility – to replenish the region's aquifer. By the 1990s, population growth made WF 21 obsolete, and OCWD developed the groundwater replenishment (GWR) system to provide tertiary wastewater treatment, replenish the aquifer, and provide 20 percent of potable supply for its service region. GWR produces 70 million gallons of freshwater per day (nearly 62 percent of northern Orange County's entire freshwater supply). Half this volume is distributed to the city of Anaheim, the largest community in the county, where it is percolated into the groundwater basin. The rest is distributed to other communities where it is injected into special groundwater wells. Project benefits include reducing the need to import and divert freshwater, lessening wastewater-generated pollution, and providing a barrier against saltwater intrusion to the aquifer. Because the recycled water is pumped and percolated underground, and then drawn from the aquifer – it is essentially "mixed" with virgin water. Most significantly, project proponents have successfully abated public concerns about wastewater re-use.

Aware of public opposition to similar efforts in Los Angeles and San Diego, OCWD also undertook a concerted public outreach effort which emphasized a four-pronged engagement and message-framing strategy. First, GWR talks were tailored to the needs, interests, and concerns of various groups. They emphasized the details of system operations, safety, and benefits. Secondly, there were numerous publications, including a brochure and website, and a public television documentary that reinforced positive images of the project. Third, the project attracted federal, state, and local grants – opened on time, and within budget. Finally, local water laws permitted recycled water uses in appropriate applications, further helping to ensure that treatment costs for non-potable applications would be manageable.

Desalination prompts another set of environmental justice challenges. While a viable technology for providing additional freshwater, its benefits and costs are unevenly distributed – making agreement regarding its implementation difficult. One of its biggest environmental justice hurdles is its potential long-term environmental impacts on local air quality and global climate. Current desalination methods consume around 14 kilowatt hours of energy for every 1,000 gallons of desalinated water produced. Given that the most common energy sources for desalination are fossil fuels, air pollution and carbon dioxide emissions are significant adverse impacts. Ironically, as a technology to augment freshwater, desalination may adversely affect long-term climate trends and, thus, regional freshwater availability.

Desalination plants also consume large amounts of land and may damage marine organisms through their intake of saline water. Heavily concentrated brine waste may kill marine organisms in the area of discharge, and the discharge is usually warmer than the surrounding water. This can upset the delicate ecological balance of marine habitats. As with wastewater re-use and demand-side management, local public perception is also an important component of environmental justice – the closer one resides to a proposed desalination facility, the higher is likely support for it.[11] In short, while desalination is a supply option, it is not a panacea.

Old and New Notions of Justice

Traditionally, environmental justice advocates have been concerned with issues such as hazardous and toxic waste storage, disposal, and incineration and their impacts on racial minorities, the poor, and women – groups upon whom the long-term intergenerational health hazards associated with these nuisances tend to fall. Environmental justice advocates also argue that access to society's most treasured environmental amenities similarly tends to be inequitably distributed, with the urban poor, racial, and ethnic minorities sharing in the fewest benefits. In most cases, traditional environmental justice conflicts tend to breed high-intensity conflict and confrontation. Worldwide, as we have seen, this traditional environmental justice paradigm remains very important for water, particularly in places such as the Central Valley where low income communities of color often lack clean water or access to improvements to address toxic contamination, the desire for inclusive participation in decisions regardless of income or race, and activities that subject indigenous peoples to cultural annihilation (e.g., dam-building and flooding ancestral lands, as we saw in the cases of Three Gorges in China).

By contrast, water conservation, IBR pricing, re-use, and desalination do not easily fit into this traditional framework for two reasons. First, the perceived benefits and risks from these innovations are socio-economically cross-cutting. While IBR and metering mostly affect lower-income communities, recycled water and desalination are perceived – fairly or not – as negatively impacting middle-class and often majority-comprised communities as well as under-represented populations. Second, impacts from all these innovations are perceived as long-term and chronic, rather than short-term and acute (e.g., community stigma, diversion of 'hard earned tax dollars' to special interests). Thus, they tend not to produce the types of political confrontations and demonstrations associated with hazardous waste, contaminated water supplies, dam-building, or regional diversion. When sudden, severe protests over water management arise, as we saw with the issue of privatization in chapter 4, it generally occurs in a specific locality where the catalyst is a discrete institution that imposes unjust and unpopular decisions (table 5.2).

We might, thus, distinguish between a traditional and a

Table 5.2   "New" and "old" notions of environmental justice and water

	Burden of impact	Characterization of hazard	Nature of conflict	Examples of disputes
Traditional notion of environmental justice and water	Risk of water problems potentially high consequence; fall on poor, women, and minorities	Threats to human health/well-being – environmental pollutants/toxic waste, reduced in-stream flow; remediation	High-intensity; social protest, violent demonstrations; acute, short-term impacts salient	Dam-building/relocating populations; inter-basin diversion; massive pollution spills
Newer idiom for environmental justice and water	Risk of water problems potentially high consequence/high uncertainty (e.g., climate change)	Broader welfare issues at stake – cost, affordability, access, actions to address/repair legacy important	Lower intensity; social protest may occur but problems viewed as long term and chronic	Wastewater re-use; desalination; involuntary conservation measures; privatizing supply

newer idiom for environmental justice and water, which both share a common denominator: the need for fair, open, and transparent decision-making processes in which all groups affected by water decisions can equally participate, and where no relevant constituency is excluded. Such processes, we argue, must embrace three characteristics. First, they must be proactive in addressing water concerns. One cannot wait for public concerns to arise. Decision makers must reach out to disaffected groups to inform them of the reasons these water-saving or supply-augmenting technologies are being endorsed, to educate and inform them, and to elicit and respond to their concerns. In regards to the three models of environmental justice discussed earlier, we can think of this first characteristic as corresponding to the covenantal tradition: everyone is presumed to have a basic right to water and to information about its quality.

Second, these innovations require that attention be paid to compensating those less able to afford the distributional burdens of IBR – this is a lesson for both private and public water vendors to bear in mind. While IBR and the benefits of metering make good sense, measures are needed to assist special populations to adopt them. Moreover, adoption should be calibrated according to affordability, and the latter is affected by factors over which the poor may have little control – such as special health needs and care for small children or the elderly. These conditions warrant a kind of categorical imperative – counter-balancing for economic hardship with low-income assistance measures, for example, and being more accessible to under-represented groups in scheduling and conducting meetings and accommodating the needs of audiences who lack the technical skill to decipher environmental documents.

Third, potable water innovations such as wastewater re-use and desalination could benefit from national-level water supply certification standards that assure protection of in-stream flow and health safeguards. These would affirm that their advantages are independently validated, and strongly resonate with the notion of stewardship.[12] Widespread adoption of these innovations will hinge on officials taking seriously calls for an ethical water policy that transcends national boundaries.

"Hard" vs. "Soft" Power

Is there evidence that water managers and other policy makers are taking seriously calls for freshwater justice? And, what would such a change look like? In recent years, there have arisen on the international environmental scene informal networks of NGOs, local and regional governance bodies, and even national government agencies who seek to collaborate toward alleviating common environmental threats to water and other resources they cannot solve by themselves.

These networks rely upon "soft power" – the ability to advance a policy agenda through convincing others to emulate certain values, policies, and even cultural attitudes that are embedded in certain prescribed measures such as local sustainability, adaptation to climate change, and the embracing of decentralized, participatory governance.

Soft power acknowledges that vulnerable states and regions realize they have no real authority to compel changes in national policy, since they are legally "wards" of more powerful national governments. However, by encouraging policy diffusion from the "bottom up;" by demonstrating, in other words, the practicality of innovative and unconventional solutions – whether a joint commission of local officials (as seen in the Israeli-Palestinian conflict), a public-private partnership (as seen in the UK), a special basin commission and set of task forces (e.g., the Chesapeake Bay, Murray-Darling basin), or a comprehensive set of voluntary cooperative protocols among NGOs, local governments, and national-level agencies (e.g., Danube and Rhine basins).

Traditionally, relations between countries that share water resources have been characterized by "hard power" relations based on asymmetries of authority over water within a given region. Sometimes called "hydro-political" regimes, these arrangements of geopolitical control afford the more powerful protagonist the ability to compel action through the granting, or the threat of withholding, economic resources such as trade, monetary exchange, or foreign assistance. While sometimes the "hegemon" can be beneficent, at other times, it may only be concerned with its own interests – creating a situation in which control skews water allocation outcomes.[13] In extreme cases, dominant powers may also rely on force or its threat. Finally, hard power is founded upon sovereign nation-states whose influence rests primarily upon internal political hierarchy and external autonomy in relations among other countries. Put another way, there is no international autarkic authority for water – governance is inherently anarchic at the global level.

While soft power has often been viewed as peripheral to resource management, beginning in the early 1990s, the United Nation's Conference on Environment and Development's (UNCED) Local Agenda 21 Program, as well as Article 10 of the Rio Declaration on Environment and Development began to encourage developing countries to restructure their national development and environmental protection plans to embrace soft power principles such as local-level decision making in environmental and resource planning. In addition, the 2000 UN Millennium Development Summit furthered the articulation of these goals for freshwater.

One anticipated payoff for countries (and their regions and cities) is greater capacity to leverage development funds in order to improve water infrastructure and make it less vulnerable to, for instance, sea-level rise. Recent international conferences that have aimed to foster more democratic water management are a reflection of this trend. The 2002 World Civil Society Forum in Geneva, Switzerland, convened a water management working group to encourage participating countries to adopt such principles as ensuring "universal access" to drinking water and bolstering a civil society sector to equitably manage water through "encouraging investment in water management . . . and ensuring that water management and conservation become everyone's business." The Forum also considered how privatization of water supply advances as well as retards the ability to bring potable water to rural populations, and whether privatization can be made democratically accountable.

The 11th Annual Stockholm Water Symposium – attended by over 1,000 water resource professionals from 150 nations in 2001 – echoed similar themes. Organized by the World Water

Council in conjunction with a number of NGOs, the symposium urged integration of water science, practice, policy and "citizen involvement." A recurring theme was financing of water infrastructure "for those in need of such development throughout the world." Attendees strongly embraced the need for local knowledge networks to check the power of private water interests by ensuring consumer protection policies, for example.

For its part, the 2000 UN Millennium Development Goals (MDGs), first articulated through its Human Development Report, and adopted by nearly 190 countries, was instrumental in defining the achievement of just, humane freshwater goals through the employment of soft power principles of partnership. Several of these goals – especially so-called "target 10," which enunciates water and sanitation improvements in developing nations, as well as a variety of other goals – have as their aim eradicating extreme poverty and improving environmental sustainability. A key feature of the MDGs is their emphasis on using household surveys, assessment questionnaires, and other local environmental and social data – including existing databases – for monitoring progress. Target 10 is actually based on a prior, 30-year-old effort supported by the World Health Organization and UNICEF called the "Joint Monitoring Programme" for measuring global water and sanitation progress.[14] Can these efforts actually succeed in making environmental justice progress?

Conclusions

Soft power goals are achievable if we are first willing to embrace fair, open and transparent decision-making processes, in which individuals and groups affected by water decisions can equally participate, and where no constituency or management approach is excluded. This seems to be the emerging lesson – and principle reason to applaud – the soft power approaches that have occurred so far. On the one hand, we must be attentive to facilitating *outcomes* that better address one's ability to pay, the affordability of water, and assurances of adequate quality and quantity. Some practical ways of meeting the "outcomes" side of the equation, underscored by our discussion of the hidden subsidies embraced in many water-saving innovations, include: stabilizing and even reversing gratuitous demands for water, discouraging profligate water use, becoming sensitive to the distributional burdens of conservation (e.g., tiered pricing, outdoor uses, water-saving appliances), and avoiding hidden water subsidies while encouraging steps such as *recycling and re-use* (e.g., making sure we are not hastening more urban growth through making available additional underpriced water).

Locally, while tiered pricing based on use should be encouraged there also need to be measures taken to assist people in the development of water infrastructure. We should encourage gradual incorporation of metering-based water charges, help alleviate local re-use system treatment costs to benefit regional supply, encourage more community-based retrofit programs, and link wastewater re-uses to local conservation and growth management strategies.

The "process" side of the reform equation is more difficult to fix. Ensuring that potable water innovations are fair and acceptable will require a larger effort to embrace these innovations within a decision-making framework that equitably considers all water management strategies as part of a "bundle" of strategies communities may consider. This is the real meaning of integrated water management discussed in chapter 4. Most of all, these innovations need to be viewed in a larger, comprehensive framework that considers all options through the same set of criteria. Three reforms are paramount: community cooperation, national-level assessment and criteria for policy, and trans-national collaboration that links networks of decision makers at all levels of governance.

First, communities must be encouraged to work together, especially when introducing costly and environmentally complex strategies for controlling demand and augmenting supply, whether diverting more water, expanding reservoir capacity, recycling wastewater, or recharging aquifers with re-used water. We know that many threats to water supply, including non-point runoff, diminished stream flow, and disputes over allocation are partly attributable to unplanned growth in water demands, growing consumptive uses, and practices that encourage wasteful water use (e.g., artificially low water prices and land use policies that subsidize urban sprawl). These practices are most directly affected by state and local decisions over land use and water management, as we saw in chapter 3.

To encourage fairness, watershed management plans must embrace multiple objectives for water, including flood control, public supply, environmental protection, navigation, power, irrigation, and industrial needs. These planning efforts should attempt to evaluate future needs, supply options, and quality/ quantity relationships as discussed in chapter 4. To effectively thwart the traditional power of entrenched, unsustainable decision-making approaches, discussed in chapters 2 and 3, national-level agencies must encourage regional cooperation. Financial assistance for water projects should be based on effective regional planning, and credit should be accorded communities that engage in broad-scale watershed planning – a reform most needed in developing societies where management of water sources and the disposal of wastewater are poorly defined processes, as in the megacities discussed in chapter 1.

These are not idle calls for justness in decisions. Internationally sponsored soft-power partnerships such as the Copenhagen Consensus have argued for employing contingent valuation studies of poor peoples' aspirations with regards to urban water system improvements – a type of preference surveying. The Consensus report notes that contrary to myth, the poor can focus on long-term needs and investments that are intended to generate benefits far into the future. Moreover, as we noted in chapter 3, recent pleas to better align governance institutions with the goals of sustainability for water and other resources are predicated precisely on overcoming political fragmentation, encouraging participation by under-represented groups, better calibrating authority for decisions with the resources needed for policy implementation, and ensuring that long-term needs and investments consistently integrate water infrastructure, energy, land use, and related decisions in a coherent fashion.[15] In this vein, multi-community (and within larger communities, multi-watershed) assessments should include studies of the appropriate role of water conservation and improved end-use efficiency as means of augmenting water supply and reducing infrastructure costs. These multi-community assessments also should consider impacts to water supply from urban sprawl and other land use practices discussed in chapters 2 and 3, and link proposals for new infrastructure to adoption of demand-side measures as well.

While growing competition over water supply has led to a global trend toward regional planning approaches to river basin management, regional planning by itself is not a panacea: national governments can promote better management of water supply, incentivize demand-side planning, and generate and enforce overall standards for water pollutants and potable water. Nation-states must take a more active role in developing planning criteria for in-stream flow, groundwater management, and water conservation – issues directly affected by climate change, agriculture, energy use, and mass migrations. Once standards are developed, it should be the task of regions to meet them through locally tailored solutions.

Second, national assessments are needed to generate consistent, reliable data for planning and to evaluate the impacts of potential climate changes on available water supply and quality; population growth and changing water use patterns on water demand; and the ecological water needs of fish and wildlife. These assessments should develop a clearinghouse of updated water information, assure and certify the quality of this information, and encourage dissemination of this information to all water users as well as public officials. Such a clearinghouse can also provide a means of validating national needs in negotiations between countries that share water sources. A similar approach is currently used in the Israeli-Palestinian Joint Water Committee (chapter 3).

Finally, at the international level, conflicts over transboundary or shared water resources will continue to resist easy efforts at shared control, as we have seen. This is compounded by the failure of countries to adequately manage internal, regional-scale problems, as in the Nile Basin, Danube, Rhine, and elsewhere. While we know that trans-boundary water problems are best managed by specialized entities that straddle watersheds, basins, and aquifers, and that combine the talents of multiple authorities, achieving cooperation will remain elusive until countries can agree on a vocabulary for equity that transcends territorial boundaries. As we have seen, this vocabulary is not impossible: if trans-national collaboration is even modestly successful, it will defuse conflict, thus benefiting all stakeholders. It will also force nations to work in ways they are not accustomed to. While soft power as a means of managing water problems is no guarantee that these problems will be managed justly, it harbors the likelihood that decisions will at least benefit the many, not just a few, and in a durable manner.

Notes

I. FRESHWATER: FACTS, FIGURES, CONDITIONS

1 Some 45 percent of Yemen's 24 million people live below the
official poverty line, and the country's literacy rate is 50 percent.
On Yemen's water problems, see: Haley Sweetland Edwards
(2009) "Yemen's water crisis builds," *Los Angeles Times*, October
11: A-22 and Jeffrey Fleishman (2009) "Yemen, on the brink
of failure, imperils region," *Los Angeles Times*, December 6:
A-28.

2 Madeline Baer (2008) "The Global Water Crisis, Privatization,
and the Bolivian Water War," pp. 195–224, in *Water, Place, and
Equity*, edited by John M. Whitely, Helen Ingram, and Richard
Warren Perry (Cambridge, MA: MIT Press). Also, "Water for Sale
– Thirst for profit: corporate control of water in Latin America"
(2009) *Council on Hemispheric Affairs*, http://www.coha.
org/2009/06/water-for-sale.

3 Alex Rodriguez (2010) "Levee breaches blamed on the rich," *Los
Angeles Times*, September 12: A-12.

4 Good discussions on Gilgel Gibe include: Lori Pottinger
(2009) "Big dam, bigger problems," *Los Angeles Times*, May 14:
A-25; one of the best analyses of Gilgel Gibe III is reported in
Ethiopia's Gibe 3 Dam: Sowing Hunger and Conflict (Berkeley,
CA: International Rivers – Report, 2009). http://www.
internationalrivers.org/node/3773. A popularized account is
found in Neil Shea (2010) "Books and guns edge out old ways
in Ethiopia's Omo Valley," *National Geographic*, 217 (3) March:
96–123. The role of development banks – both pro and con – in
the project's germination, support, and opposition, is featured
in *Gilgel Gibe III Hydro Power Project*, 2007. (Côte d'Ivoire:
African Development Bank Group). http://www.afdb.org/en/

projects-operations/project-portfolio/project. Also, see "European investment bank stops funding Gilgel Gibe III," *Abbay Media*, July 23, 2010. http://abbaymedia.com/News.

5 P. Malfatto and E.A. Vallet (2004) "Water geopolitics in North America," paper presented at the *Annual Meeting of the International Studies Association*, Le Centre Sheraton Hotel, Montreal, Quebec, Canada, March 17.

6 For a review of the anticipated – and thought-to-be already occurring – impacts to freshwater from climate change, see: D.W. Attwood, T.C. Bruneau, and J.G. Galaty (eds.) (1988) *Power and Poverty: Development and Development Projects in the Third World* (Boulder, CO: Westview Press); Peter H. Gleick, D. Briane Adams, and others (2000) *Water: The Potential Consequences of Climate Variability and Change for the Water Resources of the United States*, The Report of the Water Sector Assessment Team of the National Assessment of the Potential Consequences of Climate Change, for the US Global Change Research Program (Oakland, CA: Prepared by the Pacific Institute for Studies in Development, Environment, and Security), September; CCSP (Climate Change Science Program) (2008) Nancy Beller-Simms and Lead Authors: Helen Ingram, David Feldman, Nathan Mantua, Katharine L. Jacobs, *U.S. Climate Change Science Program Synthesis and Assessment Product 5.3 – Decision-Support Experiments and Evaluations using Seasonal to Interannual Forecasts and Observational Data: A Focus on Water Resources* (National Oceanic and Atmospheric Administration), November; S. Smith and E. Reeves (eds.) (1988) *Human Systems Ecology: Studies in the Integration of Political Economy, Adaptation, and Socionatural Regions* (Boulder, CO: Westview Press); Paul E. *Waggoner (ed.) (1990) Climate Change and U.S. Water Resources* (New York: John Wiley & Sons); IPCC (Intergovernmental Panel on Climate Change) (2007) *Climate Change 2007: The Physical Science Basis. Contribution of Working Group I to the Fourth Assessment Report of the Intergovernmental Panel on Climate Change*, edited by S. Solomon, D. Qin, M. Manning, Z. Chen, M. Marquis, K.B. Averyt, M. Tignor, and H.L. Miller (Cambridge and New York: Cambridge University Press); Jacques Leslie (2000) "Running Dry; What happens when the world no longer has enough fresh water," *Harper's Magazine*, July; P.C.D. Milly, K.A. Dunne, and A.V. Vecchia (2005) "Global pattern of trends in streamflow and

water availability in a changing climate," *Nature*, 438 (7066), 347–50.

7 Good background material on the relationship between land use, runoff, pollution, and water quality discussed in this section can be found in: K.E. Baer and C.M. Pringle (2000) "Special problems of urban river conservation: The encroaching megalopolis," pp. 385–402 in P. J. Boon, B. R. Davies, and G. E. Potts (eds.), *Global Perspectives on River Conservation: Science, Policy, and Practice* (New York: John Wiley). Also: John A. Hoornbeek (2011) *Water Pollution Policies and the American States* (Albany, NY: SUNY Press). A fuller discussion of the public health-related statistics and problems of developing nations cited in this section can be found in: *Water for People, Water for Life: the United Nations World Water Development Report – Executive Summary* (2003) (Paris: World Water Assessment Program, UNESCO Division of Water Sciences, UNESCO Publishing).

8 Excellent sources on the Athabasca oil sands case include: Robert Kunzig (2009) "The Canadian oil boom – Scraping bottom," *National Geographic*, 215 (3) March: 34–59 and Henry Vaux, Jr (2010) "Equity in policy: Failure and opportunity," *Natural Resources Journal*, 50 (2): 517–38.

9 On pharmaceutical and personal care products and their threat, see: US Environmental Protection Agency (2009) *Pharmaceuticals and Personal Care Products (PPCPs)* (Washington, DC: EPA). http://epa.gov/ppcp/.

10 Classic accounts of the emergence of so-called "hydraulic societies" include: Karl A. Wittfogel (1957) *Oriental Despotism: A Comparative Study of Total Power* (New Haven, CT: Yale University Press), and, regarding the American West, Donald Worster (1985) *Rivers of Empire: Water, Aridity, and the Growth of the American West* (New York: Oxford University Press). Also of interest are two other books by Worster: *Dust Bowl: The Southern Plains in the 1930s.* (New York: Oxford University Press, 1979), and *A River Running West: The Life of John Wesley Powell* (New York: Oxford University Press, 2001). Wittfogel's enduring description is worth repeating: "The ruling class of hydraulic society is represented first by its active core, the men of the apparatus. In virtually all hydraulic countries these men are headed by a ruler, who has a personal entourage . . . and who controls and directs his numerous civil and military underlings

through a corps of ranking officials." For his part, Worster characterized the American West as follows: "the American West can best be described as a modern *hydraulic society* . . . a social order based on the intensive, large-scale manipulation of water and its products in an arid setting. [It is] increasingly a coercive, monolithic, and hierarchical system, ruled by a power elite based on the ownership of capital and expertise."

11 See: Ariel Dinar and Shlomi Dinar (2007) "The development and application of international water law," pp. 54–76, in *Bridges Over Water: Understanding Trans-boundary Water Conflict, Negotiation, and Cooperation,* edited by A. Dinar, S. Dinar, S. McCaffrey, and D. McKinney (Hackensack, NJ: World Scientific Publishing Company).

12 On the US and Mexico, see: N.N. Gunaji (1995) "Anatomy of the extraordinary drought at the U.S.–Mexico border," *Management of Water Resources in North America III: Anticipating the 21st Century,* edited by N. Buras. Proceedings of the Engineering Foundation Conference, Tucson, AZ, September 4–8, 1993 (New York: American Society of Civil Engineers), pp. 139–48; R.W. Higgins, Y. Chen, A.V. Douglass (1999) "Internannual variability of the North American warm season precipitation regime," *Journal of Climate,* 12 (3), 653–80; and S.P. Mumme (2003) *Strengthening Binational Drought Management.* Utton Center Report: University of New Mexico School of Law, 2 (1), 3–7.

13 Good discussions of the current Nile Basin Initiative include: *Nile Basin Initiative* (2010) (http://www.nilebasin.org); "The rights to the river" (2009) *The Sustainable Water Resources e-journal,* 1 (2) August. www.waterresource.co.za/index.php?option=com_content, and Jeffrey Fleishman and Kate Linthicum (2010) "Demands on the Nile imperil Egypt's lifeline," *Los Angeles Times,* September 12: A-1, 6 and 7. More scholarly background to the dispute is afforded by John Waterbury (2002) *The Nile Basin: National Determinants of Collective Action* (New Haven, CT: Yale University Press).

14 Regarding "virtual water," see the excellent discussion in the *United Nations World Water Development Report 3: Water in a Changing World* (New York: World Water Assessment Program, 2009), chapter 2. As this report notes, a global virtual water trade could actually save water if products are traded from countries with high water productivity to countries with lower productivity.

For example, Mexico imports wheat, maize and sorghum from the US. This requires the US to use 7.1 billion m³ of water a year to produce these grains – a lot of water, certainly. However, if Mexico substituted imports by producing these same crops domestically, it would require 15.6 billion m³ of water per year, due to differences in climate, soils, and topography. Thus, from a global perspective, trade in cereals saves 8.5 billion m³ of water a year. Many countries, including Japan, Mexico and most of the nations of Europe, the Middle East and North Africa have net virtual water imports. Thus, ensuring food security in many countries strongly depends on having access to external water or food resources. In all cases, when water is used for agriculture, higher water consumption ensues – somewhere.

15 On the various ways in which water "stress" is defined, the reader is referred to several good sources, including: World Meteorological Organization (WMO) (1997) *Comprehensive Assessment of the Freshwater Resources of the World*. (Stockholm: WMO and Stockholm Environment Institute). Also, World Resources Institute (WRI) in collaboration with the United Nations Development Programme, United Nations Environment Programme, and the World Bank (1998) *World Resources 1998– 99: A Guide to the Global Environment: Environmental Change and Human Health* (New York: Oxford University Press). In general, experts define stress as: (1) the availability of water falling below a prescribed minimum (e.g., WRI, World Bank); (2) functional deficiencies in supply caused by a lack of infrastructure or fiscal resources (e.g., 1997 UN assessment); or (3) a proportional imbalance between supply and demand. The bottom line is that stress is due to a combination of population pressures, "megacity" growth, low GDP, and pressures to "internally re-allocate" water.

2. WATER: GEOPOLITICS AND SUSTAINABILITY

1 For a general review of sustainability issues regarding freshwater, the reader is referred to the A/42/427 *Our Common Future: Report of the World Commission on Environment and Development* (United Nations, 1983) World Commission on Environment and Development (1987). Presentation to UNEP's 14th Governing

Council Session, June 8. For an interesting perspective on holistically balancing economic, environmental and social concerns regarding water, see: *Connecting the Drops toward Creative Water Strategies – A Water Sustainability Tool* (2002) Global Environmental Management Initiative. Chapter 5 examines many of the subsequent freshwater reports issued by various organizations since the 1980s.

2 Table adapted from: Peter Gleick (1998) "Water in crisis: Paths to sustainable water use," *Ecological Applications*, 8: 571–9.

3 Thomas Homer-Dixon (1991) "On the threshold: Environmental changes as causes of acute conflict," *International Security*, 16 (2), Fall: 76–116.

4 John T. Scholz and Bruce Stiftel (2005) "The challenges of adaptive governance," pp. 1–11, in *Adaptive Governance and Water Conflict: New Institutions for Collaborative Planning*, edited by J. Scholtz and B. Stiftel (Washington, DC: Resources for the Future).

5 See: Wayne B. Solley, Robert R. Pierce, and Howard A. Perlman (1998) *Estimated Use of Water in the United States in 1995*, US Geological Survey, Circular 1200 (Denver, CO: US Geological Survey), p. 3 has a useful discussion of water consumption. Agriculture is not the only consumptive use of freshwater. As Solley and his colleagues note, incorporation of freshwater into manufactured products or its use by people is also consumptive, but not to the same extent. Not only is food and fiber production consumptive but, complicating matters is the fact that when water used for irrigating crops is returned to a stream, it usually occurs at a distance somewhat downstream from the point of original withdrawal. Thus, as far as the users *immediately* below the point of withdrawal are concerned, it is unavailable for their use.

6 IPCC (Intergovernmental Panel on Climate Change) (2007) "Climate Change 2007: Impacts, Adaptation, and Vulnerability," *Contribution of Working Group II to the Fourth Assessment Report of the Intergovernmental Panel on Climate Change*, edited by M.L. Parry, O.F. Canziani, J.P. Palutikof, P.J. van der Linden and C.E. Hanson (Cambridge and New York: Cambridge University Press).

7 Jyoti Thottam (2010) "How India's success is killing its Holy River: From the Himalayas to the plains, rampant growth is

turning the Ganges into a toxic sewer: it's not too late to put things right," *Time,* July 19: 28–33.

8   *United Nations World Water Development Report 3* (2009) *Chapter 2: Demographic, Economic, and Social Drivers* (Paris: World Water Assessment Program, UNESCO Division of Water Sciences, UNESCO Publishing), p. 32.

9   General analyses of the multiple impacts of climate change on freshwater, and how regional responses may worsen them, include: S. Smith and E. Reeves (eds.) (1988) *Human Systems Ecology: Studies in the Integration of Political Economy, Adaptation, and Socionatural Regions* (Boulder, CO: Westview Press); D.W. Attwood, T.C. Bruneau, and J.G. Galaty (eds.) (1988) *Power and Poverty: Development and Development Projects in the Third World* (Boulder, CO: Westview Press); E.R. Cook, C.A. Woodhouse, C.M. Eakin, and D.M. Meko (2004). "Long-term aridity changes in the western United States," *Science,* 306 (5698): 1015–18. More specific analyses on climate change and groundwater are found in: P.M. Huck (2006) "Hydrologic modeling of pathogen fate and transport," *Environmental Science and Technology,* 40 (15), 4746–53, B.J. Morehouse, R.H. Carter, and P. Tschakert (2002) "Sensitivity of urban water resources in Phoenix, Tucson, and Sierra Vista, Arizona, to severe drought," *Climate Research,* 21 (3), 283–97. Selected local cases are covered in P.J. Zarriello and K.G. Ries (2000) *A Precipitation-Runoff Model for Analysis of the Effects of Water Withdrawals on Streamflow, Ipswich River Basin, Massachusetts,* Water resources investigations report 00-4029 (Northborough, MA: USGS) (http://purl.access.gpo.gov/GPO/ LPS24844). Also, H.A. Loáiciga (2003) "Climate change and groundwater," *Annals of the Association of American Geographers,* 93 (1), 30–41; B.H. Hurd, N. Leary, R. Jones, and J.B. Smith (1999) "Relative regional vulnerability of water resources to climate change," *Journal of the American Water Resources Association,* 35 (6), 1399–410; and B. Lyon, N. Christie-Blick, and Y. Gluzberg (2005) "Water shortages, development, and drought in Rockland County, New York," *Journal of the American Water Resources Association,* 41 (6), 1457–69.

10 Energy, water and climate change is discussed in: US Department of Energy (2006) *Energy Demands on Water Resources.* Report to the Congress on the Interdependency of Energy and Water. Department of Energy, Washington, DC, available at: http://

www.sandia.gov/energy-water/congress_report.htm; S.S. Hutson, N.L. Barber, J.F. Kenny, K.S. Linsey, D.S. Lumia, and M.A. Maupin (2004) *Estimated Use of Water in the United States in 2000* (Reston, VA: US Geological Survey); and Climate Change Science Program's Synthesis and Analysis Product 4.5 examined how climate change will affect the energy sector (Nancy Beller-Simms, Helen Ingram, David Feldman, Nathan Mantua, and Katharine L. Jacobs (2008) *US Climate Change Science Program Synthesis and Assessment Product 5.3 – Decision-Support Experiments and Evaluations using Seasonal to Interannual Forecasts and Observational Data: A Focus on Water Resources.* Washington, DC: National Oceanic and Atmospheric Administration, November). The *2008 Declaration of the High-Level Conference on World Food Security: The Challenges of Climate Change and Bioenergy* cautions: "We are convinced that in-depth studies are necessary to ensure that production and use of biofuels is sustainable in accordance with the three pillars of sustainable development and takes into account the need to achieve and maintain global food security"; also, *United Nations World Water Development Report 3*, chapter 2 (2009).

11 See: Ezekiel, 47: 8–12 (New International Version). On Frontinus, see: Sextus Julius Frontinus (1997) *Frontinus: The Strategems and the Aqueducts of Rome*, English translation by C.E. Bennett (Cambridge, MA: Loeb Classical Library, Harvard University Press).

12 Terri Hathaway (2009) "Gibe 3 Dam, Ethiopia," *International Rivers.* www.international rivers.org/node/3773. See also Chapter 1, Note 4.

13 For background on the Hadejia-Jama'are-Komadugu-Yobe Basin see: Muhammad J. Chiroma, Y.D. Kazaure, Y.B. Karaye, and A.J. Gashua, "Water management issues in the Hadejia-Jama'are-Komadugu-Yobe Basin: DFID-JWL and stakeholders experience in information sharing, reaching consensus, and physical interventions," working paper. Available at: http://www.iwmi.cgiar.org/Research_Impacts/Research_Themes/BasinWaterManagement/RIPARWIN/PDFs/14%20Muhammad%20Chiroma%20SS%20FINAL%20EDIT.pdf. Also, a good study regarding water allocation and economic impacts in the region is Edward B. Barbier (2002) "Upstream dams and downstream water allocation: The case of the Hadejia'

Jama'are floodplain, Northern Nigeria," paper prepared for the Environmental Policy Forum, Centre for Environmental Science and Policy, Institute for International Studies, Stanford University, November 7, 2002.

14 On the Latin American Clean Water Initiative, see: *Partnerships for sustainable development* (2008). Available at: http://webapps01. un.org/dsd/partnerships/public/partnerships/2266.html also, http://www.resourcefnd.org. Also, see: The Resource Foundation (2010) *Case Study: Potable Water in Honduras* (New York: The Resource Foundation). Available at: http://www.resourcefnd. org/mediacenter/casestudies/175-case-study-potable-water-in-honduras.html

15 On local water management in Brazil, see: M.C. Lemos and J.L.F. Oliveira (2004) "Can water reform survive politics? Institutional change and river basin management in Ceará, Northeast Brazil," *World Development*, 32 (12), 2121–37, and M.C. Lemos and J.L.F. Oliveira (2005) "Water reform across the state/society divide: the case of Ceará, Brazil," *International Journal of Water Resources Development*, 21 (1), 93–107.

3. THREATS TO FRESHWATER

1 A good overview of the problems and pitfalls of restoration is found in Andrea K. Gerlak (2008) "Today's pragmatic water policy: Restoration, collaboration, and adaptive management along U.S. rivers," *Society & Natural Resources*, 21 (6), 538–45. Also see: Betsy A. Cody and Nicole T. Carter (2009) *35 Years of Water Policy: The 1973 National Water Commission and present challenges* (Washington, DC: Congressional Research Service), May 11.7-5700, www.crs.gov. R-40573.

2 Until the early 1800s, the Los Angeles River periodically changed its course from San Pedro Bay, south of the city, to roughly due West – through present day Santa Monica via Ballona Wash and the "cienegas," or great marshlands that lay between the Baldwin and Beverly Hills. On efforts to restore the Los Angeles River and their significance, see: Blake Gumprecht (2001) *The Los Angeles River: Its Life, Death, and Possible Rebirth* (Baltimore, MD: Johns Hopkins University Press), and Blake Gumprecht (2005) "Who killed the Los Angeles River," pp. 115–34 in *Land of Sunshine: an*

Environmental History of Metropolitan Los Angeles, edited by W. Deverell and G. Hise (Pittsburgh, PA: University of Pittsburgh Press). Early human history of the river and discussions of its management are found in Norris Hundley (2001) *The Great Thirst – Californians and Water: A History*, revised edn. (Berkeley, CA: University of California Press), and Catherine Mulholland (2000) *William Mulholland and the Rise of Los Angeles* (Berkeley, CA: University of California Press).

3 See: *Convention on the Protection of the Rhine* (http://www.iksr. org/fileadmin/user_upload/Dokumente_en/convention_on_ the_protection_of__the_rhine.pdf); *European Water Framework Directive* (http://www.iksr.org/index.php?id=148&L=3); and *Rhine 2020* (http://www.iksr.org/index.php?id=30&L=3 / http://www. iksr.org/fileadmin/user_upload/Dokumente_en/rhein2020_e. pdf). Among the industrial and environmental groups collaborating in ICPR efforts are: Birdlife International, the European Chemical Industry Council, the International Syndicate of Waterworks in the Rhine Catchment Area, the World Wide Fund for Nature, Greenpeace, the European Association of Water Suppliers and Waste Water Treatment Plants, and Alsace Nature. See: Lenard Milich and Robert G. Varady (1998) "Managing transboundary resources: Lessons from river-basin accords," *Environment*, 40, pp. 10–15, and Malcolm Newsom (1997) *Land, Water and Development: Sustainable Management of River Basin Systems*, 2nd edn. (New York: Routledge).

4 On China's Three Gorges Dam Project, see John Byrne, University of   Delaware, cited in Bruce Kennedy (1999) "China's Three Gorges Dam," *CNN.Com – Visions of China – Asian Superpower*, available at: http://www.cnn.com/SPECIALS/1999/ china.50/asian.superpower/; Alice Gibb, Northern Arizona University, quoted in: "River damming leads to dramatic decline in native fish numbers" (2008) *Science and Technology News*, July 10, available at: http://222.physorg.com/news134899161. html; International Rivers (undated) "Three Gorges Dam," available at: http://www.internationalrivers.org/china/three-gorges-dam; Jane McCartney (2007) "Three Gorges Dam is a disaster in the making, China admits," *The Sunday Times*, *London*, September 27, available at: http://www.timesonline. co.uk/tol/news/world/article2537279.ece. An excellent historical account is found in: Elizabeth C. Economy (2010) *The River Runs*

Black – the Environmental Challenge to China's Future. A Council on Foreign Relations Book (Ithaca, NY: Cornell University Press), chapter 6. Also, see: "Three Gorges Dam braces for surge of water on Yangtze as floods continue," (2010) *Bloomberg News*, July 26, available at: http://www.bloomberg.com/news/print/2010-07-26/three-gorges-dam.

5 On storm-water management as an urban problem, see Susan Lauer (2008) "Making storm-water a resource, not a problem," *The California Runoff Rundown – a Newsletter of the Water Education Foundation*, Fall: 1; 4–9; 12, and Wendy L. Manley (2008) "Storm water regulation update: Rough waters in California," *The Water Report; Water Rights, water quality, and water solutions in the West*, 55 (September 15): 1–9. Also, see: Sheldon Kameniecki and Amy Below (2009) "Ethical issues in storm water policy implementation: Disparities in financial burdens and overall benefits," pp. 69–94, in *Water, Place, and Equity*, edited by John M. Whiteley, Helen Ingram, and Richard Perry (Cambridge, MA: MIT Press). See pp. 74–5 especially. Third World impediments are discussed in *Water for People, Water for Life: the United Nations World Water Development Report – Executive Summary* (2003) (Paris: World Water Assessment Program, UNESCO Division of Water Sciences, UNESCO Publishing).

6 Defra (2008) *Future Water – The Government's Water Strategy for England* (London: The Stationery Office).

7 Jos van Gils and Joachim Bendow (2000) *The Danube Water Quality Model and its Role in the Danube River Basin Pollution Reduction Programme*, Technical Working group, ICPDR; International Commission for the Protection of the Danube River (ICPDR) (2005) *The Danube River Basin District, Part A – Basin-wide Overview* (Vienna: ICPDR), March, available at: http://www.icpdr.org/icpdr-iles/8226; http://iwhw.boku.ac.at/Donau/Environmental_Programme_Danube.pdf; http://ece.columbia.edu/research/intermarium/vol6no2/furst3.pdf. On the Black Sea, see Laurence Mee (2006) "Reviving Dead Zones: How can we restore coastal seas ravaged by runaway plant and algae growth caused by human activities?" *Scientific American* (November): 78–85. Available at: http://faculty.bennington.edu/~sherman/the%20ocean%20project/reviving%20dead%20zones.pdf

8 On Great Lakes exports, see: Stephen Handelman (2001)

"Exporting fresh water – Entrepreneurs press a reluctant Canada to let them sell its abundant eau to a thirsty world," *Time*, August 13: 14–15. On seaborne "water bags," see: Ben Smalley (2002) "Water Transport," *Al Shindagah – U.A.E.*, Issue 44 (February), available at: http://www.alshindagah.com/janfeb2002?Water_transport.html.

9 Michael Glantz (1995) "Diverting Russian rivers: An idea that won't die," *Fragilecologies*, October, available at: http://www.fragilecologies.com/oct09_95.html; Ferghana News Agency (2008) "Diverting Russian rivers to Central Asia may wreak havoc with the global temperature balance," Ferghana News Agency, Moscow, June 16, available at: http://ferghana.ru/news.php?id=402. On "glasnost" and environmental reform, see: Judith Sadaitis (2000) "Democratization in Russia under Gorbachev, 1985–1991: the birth of a voluntary sector," *Slavic Review*, 59 (3): 691–3, and Jonathan D. Oldfield (2006) *Russian Nature: Exploring the Environmental Consequences of Societal Change* (London: Ashgate).

10 Murray-Darling Basin Authority (2002) *About MDB Initiative*, Canberra City, Australia, available at: http://www.mdbc.gov.au/about/governance/agreement_history.htm; Senate Standing Committee on Science and the Environment (1979) *Continuing Scrutiny of Pollution: The River Murray*, progress report, June, Parliamentary paper 117/1979 (Canberra: Government Printer); and A. Wells (1994) *Up and Doing: A Brief History of the Murray Valley Development League, Now the Murray Darling Association, from 1944 to 1994* (Sydney: Murray Darling Association). Further information on the Murray Darling can be found in: Narelle Martin (2006) "Watershed Management in the Murray Darling Basin, Australia," pp. 51–6 in *Proceedings of the Ninth Biennial Watershed Management Council Conference*, edited by Charles W. Slaughter and Neil Berg, University of California Water Resources Center Report No. 107 (Oakland, CA: University of California).

11 Good reviews of the evolution of flood policy are found in: Jack D. Kartez (1994) "Collaboration and responsibility: Intergovernmental relationships in flood hazard management," background paper prepared for Lincoln Institute of Land Policy, Community Land Policy and River Flooding Conference; Gilbert F. White (1994) "A perspective on reducing losses from natural

hazards," *Bulletin of the American Meteorological Society*, 75 (7): 1237–41. Scott Faber (1996) *On Borrowed Land: Public Policies for Floodplains* (Cambridge, MA: Lincoln Institute of Land Policy); Upper Mississippi River Basin Association (UMRBA) (1993) *Position of the Upper Mississippi River Basin Association on Flood Response and Recovery after the 1993 Flood* (St. Paul, MN: UMRBA), September; and Subcommittee on Disaster Reduction (2005) "Grand challenges for disaster reduction," *Natural Hazards Observer*, 30 (2): 1–3. On Bangladesh, see: Simon Robinson (2007) "How Bangladesh survived a flood," *New York Times*, November 19, available at: http://www.time.com/time/world/article/0,8599,1685330,00.html#ixzz1ctqiWiPs; also, Don Belt (2011) "The coming storm," *National Geographic*, 219 (5): 58–83.

12   Good accounts of the Chesapeake Bay program and its origins are found in: Howard R. Ernst (2003) *Chesapeake Bay Blues: Science, Politics, and the Struggle to Save the Bay* (New York: Rowman & Littlefield), and *Chesapeake Bay Program – A Watershed Partnership* (2010), available at: http://www.chesapeakebay. net/; also see: Susan Olivetti Martin (2010) "Maryland's second generation of smart growth," *Planning*, 76 (3): 20–24.

13   On Itaipu Dam, see: Itaipu Binacional (2010) "Itaipu Binacional, the World's Largest Generator of renewable Clean Energy," available at: http://www.itaipu.gov.br/en/history; US Geological Survey (2010) "Itaipú Dam: The world's largest hydroelectric plant," March 29, available at: http://ga.water.usgs.gov/edu/hybiggest.html; Power Technology.com (2010) "Itaipu Hydroelectric Dam, Brazil," available at: http://www.power-technology.com/projects/itaipu-hydroelectric/.

14   Edmund Sanders (2010) "An enclave far from settled," *Los Angeles Times*, October 3: A1, 8–9; WASH News Middle East and North Africa (2009) "Palestine: FoEME calls for replacement of 'failed' Joint Water Committee," available at: http://washmena. wordpress.com/2009/05/25/palestine-foeme-calls-for. On water disputes between Israel, the Palestinian West Bank, and Gaza, see: Sharif S. Elmusa (1995) "Dividing common water resources according to international water law: The case of the Palestinian Israeli waters," *Natural Resources Journal*, 223 (Spring); Rosanna Hassoun (1998) "Water between Arabs and Israelis: Reaching twice-promised resources," pp. 313–38, in *Water, Culture, and*

Power: Local Struggles in a Global Context, edited by John M. Donahue and Barbara Rose Johnston (Washington, DC: Island Press).

15 On differences between high and low intensity disputes and their resolution, see: Ken Conca and Geoffrey D. Dabelko (2002) "The problems and possibilities of environmental peacemaking," pp. 220–34, in *Environmental Peacemaking*, edited by Ken Conca and Geoffrey D. Dabelko (Baltimore, MD: Johns Hopkins University Press); Ken Conca (2005) "Growth and fragmentation in expert networks: The elusive quest for integrated water resources management," pp. 432–70, in *Handbook of Global Environmental Politics*, edted by Peter Dauvergne (Cheltenham: Edward Elgar); and John T. Scholz and Bruce Stiftel (2005) "The challenges of adaptive governance," pp. 1–11, in *Adaptive Governance and Water Conflict: New Institutions for Collaborative Planning*, edited by J. Scholtz and B. Stiftel (Washington, DC: Resources for the Future).

4. WHO'S IN CONTROL?

1 United Nations Development Programme (2006) *Human Development Report 2006: Beyond Scarcity: Power, Poverty and the Global Water Crisis* (New York: Palgrave Macmillan).

2 Alison E. Post (2009) "Pathways for redistribution; privatization, regulation, and incentives for investment in the Argentine water sector," *International Journal of Public Policy*, 4 (1–2): 51–75.

3 David Minkow (2003) "Many Latinos favor bottled water," *The California Report – La Prensa San Diego*, February 7, available at: http://laprensa-sandiego.org/archive/february07-03/water. htm; Adrianna Quintero-Somaini and Mayra Quirindongo (2004) *Hidden Danger – Environmental Health Threats in the Latino Community* (New York; Natural Resources Defense Council); Richard Marosi (2001) "Latinos Assured Water is OK," *Los Angeles Times*, July 31, available at: http://articles. latimes.com/2001/jul/31/local/me-28784; Ed Mendel (2007) "Bill would turn up heat on bottled water," *San Diego Union-Tribune*, May 21, available at: http://legacy.signonsandiego.com/uniontrib/20070521/news

4 See: Steve Erie (2006) *Beyond Chinatown: The Metropolitan Water*

District, Growth, and the Environment in Southern California (Palo
Alto, CA: Stanford University Press). On the phenomenal growth
of privatization, see: Dale Whittington, W. Michael Hanemann,
Claudia Sadoff and Marc Jeuland (2008) *The Challenge of Water
and Sanitation* (Copenhagen, Denmark: Copenhagen Consensus
Challenge paper).

5 David Hall and Emanuele Lobina (2007) *Water Companies in
Europe, 2007.* A report commissioned by the European Federation
of Public Service Unions (EPSU) (www.epsu.org) Public Services
International Research Unit, University of Greenwich, April, p. 4.
A good discussion of the range and types of privatization activities
in the water sector is: Jessica Budds and Gordon McGranahan
(2003) "Are the debates on privatization missing the point?
Experiences from Africa, Asia, and Latin America," *Environment
and Urbanization*, 15 (2): 87–113.

6 Steve Erie (2006) *Beyond Chinatown: The Metropolitan Water
District, Growth, and the Environment in Southern California* (Palo
Alto, CA: Stanford University Press), p. 261. Also, see: EAP
Task Force for the Implementation of the Environmental Action
Program for Eastern Europe, Caucasus and Central Asia (2007)
*Financing Water Supply and Sanitation in EECCA Countries and
Progress in Achieving the Water-Related Millennium Development
Goals* (Paris: Organization for Economic Co-operation and
Development). Among the growing body of critiques of
privatization, the reader is especially referred to: Vandana Shiva
(2001) "World Bank, WTO, and corporate control over Water,"
International Socialist Review, August/September, available at:
http://www.thirdworldtraveler.com/Water/Corp_Control_Water_
VShiva.html. Also, see: Maude Barlow and Tony Clarke (2002)
Blue Gold: the Fight to Stop the Corporate Theft of the World's Water
(New York: New Press); Vandana Shiva (2009) *Water Wars:
Privatization, Pollution, and Profit* (London: Pluto Press); Maude
Barlow (2009) *Blue Covenant: The Global Water Crisis and the
Coming Battle for the Right to Water* (New York: New Press).

7 Megan Mullin (2009) *Governing the Tap: Special District
Governance and the New Local Politics of Water* (Cambridge, MA:
MIT Press), p. 9. New York was impelled toward the Croton
Watershed in Westchester County, some 64.4 km (40 miles) to
its north, by the poor quality and inadequate volume of its local
supplies. A cholera epidemic in 1832, caused in part by degraded

water quality and poor waste disposal, drove efforts to build a Croton Aqueduct. Declining well levels, which made firefighting capacity inadequate, was also a factor. See: Gerard T. Koeppel (2000) *Water for Gotham: A History* (Princeton, NJ: Princeton University Press). Also, Edward Glaeser (2011) *Triumph of the City: How Our Greatest Invention Makes us Richer, Smarter, Greener, Healthier, and Happier* (New York: Penguin Press).

8 R. Atwater and W. Blomquist (2002) "Rates, rights, and regional planning in the metropolitan water district of Southern California," *Journal of the American Water Resources Association*, 38 (5): 1195–205; Janice A. Beecher (1995) "Integrated resource planning fundamentals," *Journal of the American Water Works Association*, 87 (6): 34–48.

9 EAP Task Force for the Implementation of the Environmental Action Program for Eastern Europe, Caucasus and Central Asia (2007) *Financing Water Supply and Sanitation in EECCA Countries and Progress in Achieving the Water-Related Millennium Development Goals* (Paris: Organization for Economic Co-operation and Development); Dean A. Wheadon (1987) "Water audit reduces unaccounted-for water," *OPF*, 13 (10): 3, 6–7.

10 Pat Brennan (2009) "Severe drought and shrinking water supplies," *Orange County Register*, June 5; Claire Webb (2011) "Rate changes prompt outrage from water district customers," *Orange County Register*, February 23.

11 Brandon Winchester and Ereney Hadjigeorgalis (2009) "An institutional framework for a water market in the Elephant Butte irrigation district," *Natural Resources Journal*, 49 (Winter): 219–48.

12 A variety of recent sources on the environmental impacts, costs, and social equity implications of bottled water include: Andrea Thompson (2009) "The energy footprint of bottled water," *Live Science*, March 18, available at: http://www.livescience.com/3406-energy-footprint-bottled-water.html; Jason Green (2009) "The environmental impacts of bottled water," *The Daily Green*, July 30, available at: http://www.thedailygreen.com/environmental-news/latest/bottled-water-47091001#ixzz1eJ4XyMao; Anne Kingston (2007) "Green report: It's so not cool," *MacLean's*, May 14, available at: http://www.macleans.ca/article.jsp?content=20070514_105163; Daniel

Beekman (2011) "Corporate Accountability International says
Nestlé's marketing of 'Pure Life' bottled water to Latinos is
deceptive – Critics say the pricey bottled water is straight from the
tap," *New York Daily News*, November 2, available at: http://www.
nydailynews.com/news/corporate-acountability-international-
nestle-marketing-pure-life-bottled-water-latinos-deceptive-article-
1.971384#ixzz1eJhajPFU; David Minkow (2003) "Many Latinos
favor bottled water," *The California Report – La Prensa San Diego*,
February 7, available at: http://laprensa-sandiego.org/archieve/
february07-03/water.htm; Adrianna Quintero-Somaini and
Mayra Quirindongo (2004) *Hidden Danger – Environmental
Health Threats in the Latino Community* (New York; Natural
Resources Defense Council); Richard Marosi (2001) "Latinos
Assured Water is OK," *Los Angeles Times*, July 31, available at:
http://articles.latimes.com/2001/jul/31/local/me-28784; Ed
Mendel (2007) "Bill would turn up heat on bottled water,"
San Diego Union-Tribune, May 21, available at: http://legacy.
signonsandiego.com/uniontrib/20070521/news; Dan Shipley
(2010) "Almost half of all bottled water comes from the tap, but
costs you much more," *The Daily Green*, August 12, available
at: http://www.thedailygreen.com/environmental-news/latest/
bottled-water-47091001#ixzz1eK4OAQi1.

13 Asian Development Bank (2004) *Evaluation Highlights of 2003*
(Manila, Philippines: ADB).

14 On the Philippines case, see: Jessica Budds and Gordon
McGranahan (2003) "Are the debates on privatization missing
the point? Experiences from Africa, Asia, and Latin America,"
Environment and Urbanization, 15 (2): 87–113, especially pp. 99
and 107. Also, see for example, Marcela Olivera and Jorge Viana
(2003) "Winning the water war," *Human Rights Dialogue*, Spring:
10–11. Also: Patrick Bond (1997) "Privatization, participation
and protest in the restructuring of municipal services: grounds
for opposing World Bank promotion of 'public–private
partnerships'," originally presented at the World Bank/NGO
Dialogue on Privatization, Washington DC, reproduced for
The Water Page, www.thewaterpage.com. Also, Alison E. Post
(2009) "Pathways for re-distribution; privatization, regulation,
and incentives for investment in the Argentine water sector,"
International Journal of Public Policy, 4 (1–2): 51–75. Finally,
details on the Dalian, China case are discussed in *United Nations*

World Water Development Report 3 (2009) *Chapter 2: Demographic, Economic, and Social Drivers* (Paris: World Water Assessment Program, UNESCO Division of Water Sciences, UNESCO Publishing), p. 32; Asian Development Bank (2004) *Evaluation Highlights of 2003* (Manila, Philippines: ADB).

15 John M. Anderies, Marco A. Janssen, and Elinor Ostrom (2004) "A framework to analyze the robustness of social-ecological systems from an institutional perspective," *Ecology and Society*, 9 (1): 18–34.

5. WATER ETHICS AND ENVIRONMENTAL JUSTICE

1 Farooq Timizi (2011) "Rare victory: Pakistan wins stay order against Indian dam," *The Express Tribune – with the International Herald Tribune*, September 25, available at: http://tribune.com. pk/story/259650/court-of-arbitration-halts-construction-of-Kishanganga-dam/. Also, Lydia Polgreen and Sabrina Tavernise (2010) "Water dispute increases India-Pakistan tension," *New York Times*, July 21, available at: http://www.nytimes. com/2010/07/21/world/asia/21kashmir.html.

2 For instance, see: Peter H. Gleick (1998) "Water in crisis: Paths to sustainable water use," *Ecological Applications*, 8: 571–9. Some basic notions of environmental justice in regards to water and other resources have recently been summarized in Seth B. Shonkoff, Rachel Morello-Frosch, Manuel Pastor, and James Sadd (2009) "Minding the climate gap: Environmental health and equity implications of climate change mitigation policies in California," *Environmental Justice*, 2 (4): 173–7. Also see: David L. Feldman (1995) *Water Resources Management: In Search of an Environmental Ethic* (Baltimore, MD: Johns Hopkins University Press).

3 See: *1992 Dublin Statement on Water and Sustainable Development*, 2 at http://www.cawater-info.net/library/eng/l/dublin.pdf. Also, John Selbourne (2000) *The Ethics of Freshwater Use: a Survey* (Paris: UNESCO). The quote on international cooperation and ethics is from Kenneth Conca (2006) *Governing Water: Contentious Transnational Politics and Global Institution Building* (Cambridge, MA: MIT Press).

4 On covenants, see: United Nations (1948) *Universal Declaration*

of Human Rights, Adopted and proclaimed by General Assembly Resolution 217 A (III) 1948 Preamble, available at: http://www. un.org/Overview/rights.html.

5 See: Wild and Scenic Rivers Act, P.L. 90-542, as amended, 16 U.S.C. 1271–1287 (1968). Also, see: Immanuel Kant, (1975) *Foundations of the Metaphysics of Morals,* translated by Lewis Beck (Indianapolis, IN: Bobbs-Merrill).

6 Aldo Leopold (1949) *A Sand County Almanac* (Oxford: Oxford University Press). Also, see: Endangered Species Act of 1973, P.L. 93-205, as amended – approved December 28, 16 U.S.C. 1531–1544, 87 Stat. 884: sections 2, 3, and 4.

7 On the subject of water rights, and the UN Commission on Science and Technology, see: John Selbourne (2000) *The Ethics of Freshwater Use: A Survey* (Paris, UNESCO): 2. On the World Water Forum and water as a human right, see: "Corporate Interests Challenged at World Water Forum," March 16, 2009, available at: http://www.alternet.org/water/131755/ corporate_interests_challenged_at_world_water_forum/. Also, see "Corporate water barons indifferent to running water but not security at World Water Forum," March 19, 2009, available at: http://www.alternet.org/blogs/water/132359/corporate_ water_barons_indifferent to_running_water_but_not_security_ at_world_water_forum/. Survival International (2009) "The most inconvenient truth of all – climate change and indigenous people," available at http://assets.survivalinternational.org/ documents/132/survival_climate_change_report_english. pdf; also, J.G Timmerman and Francesca Bernardini (2009) *Perspectives on Water and Climate Change Adaptation – Adapting to Climate Change in Transboundary Water Management* (World Water Council and IUCN). See: Oxfam International (2009) *Oxfam's Commitment to Human Rights,* available at: http://www. oxfam.org/en/about/why; also, see International Rivers (2009) "Mission," available at http://www.internationalrivers.org/en/ mission. Also, see: Report of the World Commission on Dams (2000) *Dams and Development: a New Framework for Decision-Making.* Finally, criticisms of the rights approach are found in: Mary Ann Glendon (1991) *Rights Talk: The Impoverishment of Political Discourse* (New York: Free Press), p. 12, and "Ethics, Human Rights, Water Management," unpublished manuscript, September 1, 2010 (New York: Ethics and Water Group).

Regarding indigenous and Western rights concepts, see; Xavier Mena V (1998) "The rights of indigenous people over their territories and natural resources," pp. 70–6, in *Searching for Equity – Conceptions of Justice and Equity in Peasant Irrigation*, edited by Rutgerd Boelens and Gloria Davila (Assen, The Netherlands: Van Gorkum & Co.).

8 For metering and demand-side management experience, see: A. Post (2006) "The paradoxical politics of water metering in Argentina," *Poverty in Focus – International Policy Centre for Inclusive Growth*, 18 (August), Poverty Practice, Bureau for Development Policy, UNDP, Brasilia, Brazil, pp. 16–18; B. Barraqué (1992) "Water Management in Europe: Beyond the Privatisation Debate," *Flux*, Paris (January–March), 7. Also, E. Hanak and M. Davis (2006) *Lawns and Water Demand in California* (San Francisco, CA: Public Policy Institute of California); D. Baumann, J. Boland, and Michael W. Hanemann (1997) *Urban Water Demand Management and Planning* (New York: McGraw-Hill); C.B. Freeman (2008) *California's Water: An LAO Primer* (Sacramento, CA: Legislative Analyst's Office), October; and E. Hanak, J. Lund, A. Dinar, B. Gray, R. Howitt, J. Mount, P. Moyle, and B. Thompson (2010) "Myths of California Water – Implications and Reality," *West and Northwest*, 16 (1), 3–74.

9 On national water use, see United Nations Development Program (UNDP) (2006) *Human Development Report 2006* (New York: UNDP), available at: www.data360.org. On fairness, affordability, and equity, see: B. Raucher (2004) "Affordability of water service: What does it mean? How is it measured? Why does it matter?" in *EFAB Affordability Workshop*, San Francisco, CA, August 18; P. Brennan (2009) "Severe drought and shrinking water supplies," *Orange County Register*, June 5, pp. 1–26; and S. M. Wilson (2007) *Assessment of Water Utility Low-Income Assistance Programs*, California Public Utilities Commission, Division of Water and Audits, Sacramento, October.

10 J. Boberg (2005) *Liquid Assets: How Demographic Changes and Water Management Policies Affect Freshwater Resources* (Report-MG-358-CF) (Santa Monica, CA: RAND Corporation). On desalination generally, see: US Geological Survey (USGS) (2010) *Water Science for Schools. Thirsty, How 'Bout a Cool, Refreshing Cup of Seawater?*, available at: http://ga.water.usgs.gov/edu/drinkseawater.html.

11 California experience with wastewater re-use is found in: *The OCWD/OCSD Partnership* (2004). Available at: http://www.gwrsystem.com/about-gwrs/facts-and-figures/theocwdocsdpartnership.html. Also, W.R. Mills, Jr., S. Bradford, M. Rigby, and M. Wehner (1998) "Groundwater recharge at the Orange County Water district," *Wastewater Reclamation and Reuse*, edited by T. Asano (Boca Raton, FL: Water Quality Management Library), vol. 10: 1105–36. On desalination justice-related issues, see: Green Living Tips (2010) *The Cost of Desalination*, available at: http://www.greenlivingtips.com/blogs/138/The-cost-ofdesalination.html; also, G. Pitzer (2009) "Desalination: a drought proof supply?" *Western Water Magazine*, July/August, available at: http://www.watereducation.org/doc.asp?id=872.

12 G.W. Miller (2011) "Integrated concepts in water reuse; managing global water needs," *Desalination*, 187: 65–75.

13 On soft power and global management of water and other resource issues, see: John Waterbury (2002) *The Nile Basin: National Determinants of Collective Action* (New Haven, CT: Yale University Press); Mark Zeitoun and Jeroen Warner (2006) "Hydro-hegemony – a framework for analysis of trans-boundary water conflicts," *Water Policy*, 8 (5): 435–60; Hendrik Spruyt (1994) *The Sovereign State and its Competitors* (Princeton, NJ: Princeton University Press); Joseph Nye, Jr. (2004) *Soft Power: The Means to Success in World Politics* (Cambridge, MA: Perseus Books). For hard power, see: Elmusa Sharif (1995) "Dividing common water resources according to international water law: The case of the Palestinian Israeli waters," *Natural Resources Journal*, 223 (Spring); Rosanna Hassoun (1998) "Water between Arabs and Israelis: Reaching twice-promised resources, pp. 313–38 in *Water, Culture, and Power: Local Struggles in a Global Context*, edited by John M. Donahue and Barbara Rose Johnston (Washington, DC: Island Press).

14 These international discussions are found in M. Grubb et al. (1993) *The Earth Summit Agreements: A Guide and Assessment – An Analysis of the Rio '92 UN Conference on Environment and Development* (London: Royal Institute of International Affairs, Earthscan Publications). UN millennium goals and water are discussed in World Water Council/World Water Forum (2010) *Water and Millennium Development Goals*, available at: http://www.worldwatercouncil.org/index.php?id=744.

15 Dale Whittington, W. Michael Hanemann, Claudia Sadoff, and Marc Jeuland (2008) *The Challenge of Water and Sanitation* (Copenhagen, Denmark: Copenhagen Consensus Challenge paper), p. 42. On aligning governance with the goal of sustainability, see: United Nations Environment Programme (2012) *21 Issues for the 21st Century – Results of the UNEP Foresight Process on Emerging Environmental Issues*, edited by J. Alcamo and S.A. Leonard (Nairobi: UNEP), pp. 6–7.

Selected Readings

Readers looking for an extended discussion on the disposition of global freshwater discussed in **chapter 1**, the sources of misunderstanding regarding its vulnerability, and the various ways in which water "stress" is defined, are referred to several good sources, including: World Meteorological Organization (WMO) (1997) *Comprehensive Assessment of the Freshwater Resources of the World* (Stockholm: WMO and Stockholm Environment Institute). Also, World Resources Institute (WRI) in collaboration with the United Nations Development Programme, United Nations Environment Programme, and the World Bank (1998) *World Resources 1998–99: A Guide to the Global Environment: Environmental Change and Human Health* (New York: Oxford University Press).

As noted in chapter 1, various definitions of stress have been offered by water experts: (1) the availability of water falling below a prescribed minimum (e.g., WRI, World Bank); (2) functional deficiencies in supply caused by a lack of infrastructure or fiscal resources (e.g., 1997 UN assessment); or (3) proportional imbalance between supply and demand. The bottom line is that stress is due to a combination of population pressures, "megacity" growth, low GDP, and pressures to "internally re-allocate" water. As a consequence, water stress results from an imbalance between water use and water resources. Its persistence causes deterioration of freshwater resources in terms of quantity (aquifer over-exploitation, dry rivers, etc.) and quality (e.g., eutrophication, organic matter pollution, saline intrusion). See, especially, Joseph Alcamo, Petra Doll, Thomas Henrichs, Frank Kaspar, Bernhard Lehner, Thomas Rosch, and Stefan Siebert (2003) "Development and testing of the WaterGAP 2 global model of water use and availability," *Hydrological Sciences – Journal des Sciences Hydrologiques*, 48 (3): 317–37, and World Water Council (2005) *Water Crisis*, available at: www.worldwater-council.org/index.php?id=25.

As a follow-up to the Bolivian case, there have been a number of contemporary accounts of water problems that take as their point of departure the threat of global geopolitical control of water by private corporations, and which examine the significance of this pattern of control in maintaining poverty and sustaining environmental injustice. Among the more important and critical of these works are Vandana Shiva (2001) "World Bank, WTO, and Corporate Control over Water," *International Socialist Review*, August/September, available at: http://www.thirdworldtraveler.com/Water/Corp_Control_Water_VShiva.html. For other popular accounts, see: Maude Barlow and Tony Clarke (2002) *Blue Gold: the Fight to Stop the Corporate Theft of the World's Water* (New York: New Press); Vandana Shiva (2009) *Water Wars: Privatization, Pollution, and Profit* (London: Pluto Press); Maude Barlow (2009) *Blue Covenant: The Global Water Crisis and the Coming Battle for the Right to Water* (New York: New Press). Also of interest on the subject of "hydraulic society" in the American West are two other books by Worster: *Dust Bowl: The Southern Plains in the 1930s* (New York: Oxford University Press, 1979), and *A River Running West: The Life of John Wesley Powell* (New York: Oxford University Press, 2001). Also, see: Council on Hemispheric Affairs (2009) "Water for Sale – Thirst for profit: corporate control of water in Latin America," available at: http://www.coha.org/2009/06/water-for-sale.

Additional background material on the relationship

between land use and water quality – and the impacts of this relationship upon environmental quality – can be found in: K.E. Baer and C.M. Pringle (2000) "Special problems of urban river conservation: The encroaching megalopolis," pp. 385–402, in P.J. Boon, B.R. Davies, and G.E. Potts (eds.), *Global Perspectives on River Conservation: Science, Policy, and Practice* (New York: John Wiley); Catherine M. Pringle (2000) "Threats to U.S. public lands from cumulative hydrologic alterations outside of their boundaries," *Ecological Applications*, 10 (4): 971–89; David M. Rosenberg, Patrick McCully, and Catherine M. Pringle (2000) "Global-scale environmental effects of hydrological alterations: Introduction," *BioScience*, 50 (9): 746–51. On urban sprawl and water, see: Dolores Hayden and Jim Wark (2004) *A Field Guide to Sprawl* (New York: W.W. Norton), and John Preston Brooks (2001) "Land use planning in karst and recharge zones," *Land and Water*, 45 (3): 26–29.

More than two-thirds of the world's urban residents live in cities in Africa, Asia, and Latin America, and since 1950 the urban population of these regions has grown five-fold. David Satterthwaite (2000) "Will most people live in cities?" *British Medical Journal*, 321 (7269): 1143–5, available at: http://www.pub medcentral.nih.gov/articlerender.fcgi?artid+1118907; also, see United Nations Population Fund (UNFPA) (2007) *State of World Population 2007: Unleashing the Potential of Urban Growth* (New York: United Nations Population Fund).

On the large and growing literature on mega-cities and freshwater, see: K.O. Adekalu, J.A. Osunbitan, and O.E. Ojo (2002) "Water sources and demand in South Western Nigeria: implications for water development planners and scientists," *Technovation*, 22: 799–805; T. Downs, M. Mazari-Hiriart, R. Dominguez-Mora, and H. Suffet (2000) "Sustainability of least cost policies for meeting Mexico City's future water demand," *Water Resources Research*, 36 (8): 2321–39; H.

Furumai (2008) "Rainwater and reclaimed wastewater for sustainable urban water use," *Physics and Chemistry of the Earth*, 33: 340–6; M. Gandy (2008) "Landscapes of disaster: water, modernity, and urban fragmentation in Mumbai," *Environment and Planning*, 40: 108–30; C. Tortajada and E. Casteian (2003) "Water management for a megacity: Mexico City metropolitan area," *Ambio*, 32 (2): 124–9; B. Maranon (2005) "Private-sector participation in the management of potable water in Mexico City, 1992–2002," *Water Resources Development*, 21 (1): 165–79; K.A. Yusuf (2007) "Evaluation of groundwater quality characteristics in Lagos City," *Journal of Applied Sciences*, 7 (13): 1780–4; and M.H. Zérah (2008) "Splintering urbanism in Mumbai: Contrasting trends in a multilayered society," *Geoforum*, 39 (2008): 1922–32.

The reader should be reminded that North America also has two major megacities, both of which have faced serious water problems throughout their history: Los Angeles and New York. On Los Angeles, see Norris Hundley, Jr. (2001) *The Great Thirst – Californians and Water: A History* (Berkeley, CA: University of California Press); Los Angeles Department of Water and Power (2010a) *Urban Water Management Plan*, available at: www.ladwp.com; Catherine Mulholland (2002) *William Mulholland and the Rise of Los Angeles* (Berkeley, CA: University of California Press); and Louis Sahagun (2009) "In the Owens Valley, resentment again flows with the water," *Los Angeles Times*, May 16: B-1. For New York City, some good sources include: Gerard T. Koeppel (2000) *Water for Gotham: A History* (Princeton, NJ: Princeton University Press); Gerard T. Koeppel (2001) *The Water Supply of New York City*, available at: http://www.gothamcenter.org/festival/2001/confpapers/koeppel.pdf and New York City (2011) *History of New York City Water Supply*, available at: http://www.nyc.gov/html/dep/html/drinking_water/history.shtml. Also, Edward Glaeser (2011) *Triumph of the City: How Our Greatest Invention Makes us Richer, Smarter, Greener, Healthier, and Happier* (New York: Penguin Press); US Environmental Protection Agency (US EPA) (2010) *Water Sense – New York Water Fact Sheet*. EPA 832-F-10-104, June, available at: www.epa.gov/watersense; Harold Shultz (2007) *Some Facts on the New York City Water and Sewer Supply System* (New York: Citizens' Housing and Planning Council).

There is a large and growing literature on adaptive management and water – a subject briefly discussed in **chapter 2**. A good overall source is: National Research Council (2004) *Adaptive Management for Water Resources Project Planning*, Panel on Adaptive Management for Resource Stewardship, Committee to Assess the US Army Corps of Engineers Methods of Analysis and Peer Review for Water Resources Project Planning, Washington, DC; and Kai N. Lee (1999) "Appraising adaptive management," *Conservation Ecology*, 3 (2): 3. On stakeholder partnerships and adaptive water management, see: William D. Leach, Neil W. Pelkey, and Paul A. Sabatier (2001) "Stakeholder partnerships as collaborative policymaking: Evaluation criteria applied to watershed management in California and Washington," *Journal of Policy Analysis and Management*, 21 (4): 645–70.

On social-ecological models and water management, see: John M. Anderies, Marco A. Janssen, and Elinor Ostrom (2004) "A framework to analyze the robustness of institutions in social-ecological systems from an institutional perspective," *Ecology and Society*, 9 (1): 18–34. Also, on the general conformance of institutional management schemes and resources, see: Jude Isabella (1999) "A turbulent industry: Fishing in British Columbia," *Journal of the Maritime Museum of British Columbia*, 45, Spring: 1–9, available at: www.goldseal.ca/wild-salmon/salmon_history.asp?article=3>; also M.J. Peterson (1992) "Whales, cetologists, environmentalists, and the international management of whaling," *International Organization*,

46 (1): 147–86. An older but no less regarded treatise on the same subject, and an excellent and insightful work is: John Wesley Powell (1879) *Lands of the Arid Region of the United States* (Washington, DC: Government Printing Office).

Chapter 3 features a couple of examples of inter-basin diversion (or, inter-basin transfer). Historical accounts of inter-basin transfers and water diversion schemes and their impacts are found in John Bright (2000) *A History of Israel* (Westminster: John Knox Press), and Philip L. Fradkin (1996) *A River No More: The Colorado River and the West* (Berkeley, CA: University of California Press). Also, see David L. Feldman and Jill Elmendorf (2000) *Water Supply Challenges Facing Tennessee: Case Study Analyses and the Need for Long-Term Planning*, prepared for the Environmental Policy Office, Tennessee Department of Environment and Conservation, by the Energy, Environment and Resources Center, University of Tennessee, Nashville, TN, June. On the Garrison Diversion Unit, see: David L. Feldman (1991) "The Great Plains Garrison Diversion Unit and the search for an environmental ethic," *Policy Sciences*, 24 (1): 41–64.

For more information on various systems of water law and their relevance for water marketing, the reader is referred to the following sources: Dan Tarlock, J.N. Corbridge, Jr., and D.H. Getches (1993) *Water Resource Management: A Casebook in Law and Public Policy*, 4th edn. (Westbury, NY: Foundation Press); Jan G. Laitos and Joseph P. Tomain (1992) *Energy and Natural Resources Law in a Nutshell* (St. Paul, MN: West Publishing); *Water in the West: Challenge for the Next Century* (1998) Report of the Western Water Policy Review Advisory Commission (Springfield, VA: NTIS), June; and Kenneth R. Wright (ed.) (1998) *Water Rights of the Eastern United States* (Denver, CO: American Water Works Association). Discussions of riparianism and water transfers are found in Lynda L. Butler (1990) "Environmental water rights: An evolving concept of public property," *Virginia Environmental Law Journal*, 9: 323–7; David M. Gillilan and Thomas C. Brown (1997) *Instream Flow Protection: Seeking a Balance in Western Water Use* (Washington, DC: Island Press); Douglas L. Grant (1998) "Introduction to Interstate Allocation Problems," *Waters and Water Rights*, edited by Robert E. Beck (Charlottesville, VA: Michie).

On water markets, prior appropriation laws, public acceptability, and fairness, see Natural Resources Law Center (1997) *Restoring the Waters* (Boulder, CO: Natural Resources Law Center, the University of Colorado School of Law, May); S. Ansley Samson and Sydney Bacchus (2000) "Point-water marketing: The other side of the coin," *Water Resources Impact*, 2 (6): 15–16; A. Dan Tarlock (1997 and 1998 update) *Law of Water Rights and Resources* (Deerfield, IL: Clark, Boardman and Callaghan); Sean P. Keenan, Richard S. Kranich, and Michael S. Walker (1999) "Public perceptions of water transfers and markets: Describing differences in water use communities," *Society and Natural Resources*, 12: 279–92; Douglas S. Kenney, S. T. McAllister, W.H. Caile, and J.S. Peckham (2000) *The New Watershed Source Book – A Directory and Review of Watershed Initiatives in the Western US* (Boulder, CO: Natural Resources Law Center, University of Colorado School of Law, April); and Clay J. Landry (2000) "Agriculture and water markets in the new millennium," *Water Resources Impact*, 2 (3): 13–15.

Good, accessible discussions on the importance of investments in water supply infrastructure discussed in **chapter 4** are found in: United Nations (2009) *UN World Water Development Report: 3 – Water in a Changing World*, World Water Assessment Program, chapter 3: 62; Rene Coulomb (2001) "Speech presented by the vice president of the World Water Council at the Closing Session of the 11th Stockholm Water Symposium," *World Water Council – 3rd World Water*

Forum – Stockholm Water Symposium, August 16, available at: www.worldwatercouncil.org, and Global Water Intelligence (2004) *Tariffs: Half Way There* (Oxford: Global Water Intelligence).

Basic discussions of the principles of integrated resource planning for water utilities are found in: David R. Warren, G.T. Blain, F.L. Shorney, and L.J. Klein (1995) "IRP: A case study from Kansas," *Journal of the American Water Works Association*, 87 (6): 57–71; Gary Fiske and Anh Dong (1995) "IRP: A case study from Nevada," *Journal of the American Water Works Association*, 87 (6): 72–83; and William W. Wade (2001) "Least-cost water supply planning," *Presentation to the Eleventh Tennessee Water Symposium*, Nashville, TN, April 15.

Comparative data on the consumer cost of water are not easy to come by. One of the most easily accessible sources is found, circa 2000, in Table 4, "Comparison of water pricing in developed countries," p. 27, in UN (2003) *Water for People, Water for Life: the United Nations World Water Development Report – Executive summary* (Paris: UNESCO-WWAP).

The charge that international organizations which serve as global forums for water issues tend to be more concerned with the interests of private water vendors than the needs of average citizens is found in a variety of sources, including: "Corporate Interests Challenged at World Water Forum," March 16, 2009, available at: http://www.alternet.org/water/131755/corporate _interests_challenged_at_world_water_forum/; "Corporate Water Barons Indifferent to Running Water But Not Security at World Water Forum," March 19, 2009, available at: http://www.alternet.org/blogs/water/132359/corpor ate_water_barons_indifferent_to_running_water_but_not_se curity_at_world_water_forum/; "Water Rights Activists Blast World Water Forum as 'Corporate Trade Show to Promote Privatization'," March 23, 2009; available at: http://www. alternet.org/water/133048/water_rights_activists_blast_world_

water_forum_as_%22corporate_trade_show_to_promote_pri
vatization%22/; and "Fixing Our Water Crisis Can't Be
Done by the Corporations that Are Exacerbating It," April 2,
2009, available at: http://www.alternet.org/water/134802/
fixing_our_water_crisis_can%27t_be_done_by_the_corpora
tions_that_are_exacerbating_it/.

On the subject of political accountability and privatization
of water services, see: Craig Anthony (Tony) Arnold (2005)
"Privatization of public water services: The states' role in
ensuring public accountability," *Pepperdine Law Review*, 32
(3): 561–604; and C.A. Arnold (2009) "Water privatization
trends in the United States: Human rights, national security, and public stewardship," *William & Mary Environmental
Law and Policy Review*, 33, p. 785–849; and Ben Crow and
Sultana Farhana (2002) "Gender, class, and access to water:
Three cases in a poor and crowded delta," *Society and Natural
Resources*, 15 (8): 709–24.

There is a growing body of literature on the socio-economic
and public health disparities associated with bottled water
use. On the issue of bottled water and minority groups, some
popular press and scholarly sources worth perusing include:
Cheryl Mendoza (2001) "Perrier is determined to set up shop
in the Great Lakes," *Great Lakes News*, 15 (1): 1–3. On bottled
water use and tap water distrust, see, especially: W.L. Hobson,
M.L. Knochel, and C.L. Byington (2007) "Bottled, filtered, and
tap water use in Latino and non-Latino children," *Archives
of Pediatric and Adolescent Medicine*, (161) 5: 457–61; Elena
Gaona (2005) "Tapping into Latinos' water fears," *San Diego
Union-Tribune*, August 6, available at: http://www.ewg.org/
node/17786; and Doug Irving (2010) "Toxic water threatens
Santa Ana neighborhood," *Orange County Register*, May 16: 3.

Some basic notions of environmental justice in regards to
water resources management discussed in **chapter 5** are summarized in Helen Ingram, David L. Feldman, and John M.

Whiteley (2008) "Water and equity in a changing climate," pp. 271–308, in *Water, Place, and Equity*, edited by J. M. Whiteley, H. Ingram, and R.W. Perry (Cambridge, MA: MIT Press). The reader is reminded that "ethics" as employed in discussions of water resources and other natural resource issues and problems has a meaning beyond that of axiology and morals – spiritual and even cultural notions of "right" and "wrong" have often been invoked in debates regarding water ethics. See, for example: Joachim Blatter and Helen Ingram (2001) *Reflections on Water: New Approaches to Transboundary Conflicts and Cooperation* (Cambridge, MA: MIT Press); also, Gary Chamberlain (2008) *Troubled Waters: Religion, Ethics, and the Global Water Crisis* (Lanham, MD: Rowman & Littlefield).

The role of ethics and conceptions of fairness in the Endangered Species Act is treated in Robert T. Lackey, "Restoring Wild Salmon to the Pacific Northwest: Framing the risk question," pp. 3–11, in *Proceedings of the Ninth Biennial Watershed Management Council Conference*, University of California Water Resources Center Report No. 107, edited by Charles W. Slaughter and Neil Berg (Oakland, CA: University of California Water Resources Center), August.

A judicious assessment of the issues associated with desalination in the US context includes some recent articles on a proposed facility near Carlsbad, California. Discussion of the project's details can be found in: Gary Pitzer (2009) "Desalination: A drought proof supply?" *Western Water Magazine*, July/August, available at: http://www.watereducation.org/doc.asp?id=872. Other accounts include, Poseidon Resources (2009) *The Carlsbad Desalination Project brought to you by Poseidon Resources*, available at: http://www.carlsbad-desal.com; Teri Sforza (2009) "Public agency to pay for desalination – Metropolitan water district will cough up $350 million to Poseidon Resources for San Diego project," *Orange County Register*, November 15: 1, 18; Sabrina Shankman (2009)

"California gives desalination plants a fresh look," *Wall Street Journal*, July 10, available at: http://online.wsj.com/article/SB124708765072714061.html#printMode.

For an expanded discussion of the various ways "soft power" is used in international resource management debates, see the following: Jan Schneider (1979) *World Public Order of the Environment: Towards an International Ecological Law and Organization* (Buffalo: University of Toronto Press); James N. Rosenau (1992) "Governance, order and change in world politics," in *Governance without Government*, edited by J. Rosenau and E.O. Czempiel (Cambridge: Cambridge University Press). Also, ICLEI (1995) Municipal leaders' communiqué to the Conference of the parties to the UN Framework Convention on Climate Change, Berlin, Germany, March; "ICLEI's climate resilient communities program addresses adaptation, vulnerabilities," ICLEI – Local Governments for Sustainability, April 11, 2007, available at: http://www.iclei.org/index.php?id=1487&tx_ttnews.

The continuing efficacy of "hard power," particularly with regards to international water policy, is discussed by Mary E. Morris (1993) *Dividing the Waters: Reaching Equitable Water Solutions in the Middle East*, RAND/P-7840 (Santa Monica, CA: RAND Corporation), Jan Selby (2003) *Water, Power, and Politics in the Middle East: the Other Israeli-Palestinian Conflict* (London: I.B. Tauris). Also, see: Mary E. Morris (1992) "Poisoned wells: The politics of water in the Middle East," reprinted from *Middle East Magazine*, RAND/RP-139 (Santa Monica, CA: RAND Corporation); Michael B. Oren (2003) *Six Days of War: June 1967 and the Making of the Modern Middle East* (New York: Random House); and Benny Morris (2008) *1948: The First Arab-Israel War* (New Haven, CT: Yale University Press).

Index